Bless you —
Charles L. Allen

From Mary & Sammy
Christmas 1966

THE SERMON ON THE MOUNT

By Charles L. Allen:

THE
SERMON
ON THE
MOUNT

Charles L. Allen

FLEMING H. REVELL COMPANY
WESTWOOD, NEW JERSEY

COPYRIGHT © 1966 BY FLEMING H. REVELL COMPANY ● ALL RIGHTS RESERVED ● WESTWOOD, NEW JERSEY ● LIBRARY OF CONGRESS CATALOG CARD NUMBER: 66-21902 ● PRINTED IN THE UNITED STATES OF AMERICA ● 1.1

To

CHARLES L. WALLIS
PROFESSOR AT KEUKA COLLEGE AND
MINISTER OF THE COLLEGE CHURCH (BAPTIST)
KEUKA PARK, NEW YORK

HARRISON McMAINS
MINISTER OF THE FIRST CHRISTIAN CHURCH
HUNTSVILLE, ALABAMA

RONALD R. MEREDITH
MINISTER OF THE FIRST METHODIST CHURCH
WICHITA, KANSAS

*Their ministry and close personal friendship
bless my life and warm my heart*

Things That Never Change

"THIS CHANGING WORLD" is a phrase we hear often. As we compare our day with Jesus' day, we do see many changes. The styles of our clothes today are very different from the long, flowing robe which Jesus wore. In His day, the preparation and cooking of foods was a very crude process, and menus were very simple. Today we have our supermarkets, which contain frozen foods, bakery bread, and a vast variety of other things to eat. Today one could probably fly all the way around the world in a jet airplane quicker than Mary and Joseph made the journey from Nazareth to Bethlehem on the back of a donkey. We press a button and flood our houses with electric light, while in Jesus' day light in the home at night was a dim thing at best. We speak a different language than He spoke. One could write at length about the changes which have taken place in our society during the last two thousand years.

On the other hand, there are many things that have never changed. The law of gravitation is the same as it was in the beginning. The four seasons come and go as they always have. The tides of the oceans rise and fall as they have done since there have been oceans. The Ten Commandments have not changed since Moses' day; stealing is still stealing. God has not changed. Henry F. Lyte expressed the faith of multitudes when he wrote: "O Thou, who changest not, abide with me." We Christians believe the author of Hebrews was correct in saying, "Jesus Christ the same yesterday, and to day, and for ever" (HEBREWS 13:8).

Neither has man really changed. Man's hopes, fears,

· 7

sorrows, happiness are the same today as they have been down through the centuries of history. The basic principles of human life have not changed.

If Jesus lived today in the flesh, rode in jet airplanes, watched television, lived in an air-conditioned home, had all the information which scientists have gained in reference to outer space, and had access to all of today's scientific knowledge, He still would not need to change one word of the Sermon on the Mount. The words which He spoke are eternal and apply equally to every age and to every generation. In fact, He Himself felt that His words were even more enduring than this universe. He said, "Heaven and earth shall pass away: but my words shall not pass away" (MARK 13:31). Therefore, when we study the Sermon on the Mount, we may be sure that it applies to our day and to each one of us.

Here I would like to express deep personal appreciation for Mrs. Helen Frazier, my secretary, who has helped so much and in so many ways in the preparation of this manuscript. Because of her broad educational background, her technical skill, and her genuine interest, she has helped me more than I could possibly measure. I appreciate her very much.

To my wife, Leila, I owe more than I owe to any other person. Not only this manuscript, but my entire ministry, would be so much poorer were it not for her.

CHARLES L. ALLEN

First Methodist Church
Houston, Texas

CONTENTS

THE SERMON ON THE MOUNT

I

I

I

The Master Teaches

THE SERMON ON the Mount is recorded in the fifth, the sixth, and the seventh chapters of the Gospel According to St. Matthew. Before the actual words of the sermon are begun, St. Matthew sets down in two short verses the basic and important principles which must be understood before one can understand the words of our Lord in the Sermon:

And seeing the multitudes, he went up into a mountain: and when he was set [sat down], his disciples came unto him: And he opened his mouth, and taught them saying . . . (MATTHEW 5:1, 2).

. . . seeing the multitudes . . .—With infinite love and compassion our Lord understood the human predicament. He had deep empathy with people; He saw their needs, their weaknesses, their desires, and their hurts. He understood and was concerned for people. Every word He spoke was uttered because He saw a need for that word in some human life. His concern was always to uplift and never to tear down, to heal and never hurt, to save and not condemn.

But notice, this Sermon on the Mount was not delivered to the multitudes. Instead Jesus withdrew Himself from them, and went out upon a mountain, where later His disciples came to Him. It is very important to know that this sermon was given first to the disciples. In nearly every church, when one is ordained into the ministry there is an ordination sermon, laying down the principles of life for the young minister. The Sermon on the Mount may be described as the ordination sermon for the twelve disciples; and beyond them the commission for every Christian who goes out to live His life and do His work. Likely the Sermon on the Mount followed very soon after our Lord chose the twelve disciples. This certainly is clearly indicated in the sixth chapter of Saint Luke's Gospel: beginning with the thirteenth verse, we have recorded the names of the twelve whom He called; then follow immediately the words of the Sermon on the Mount.

This is very important for us to see, because today we have a dangerous tendency of thinking of our Lord as a teacher before we think of Him as the Saviour. This can be a fatal mistake. Without our knowing Christ as the Saviour, His teachings can be so beyond our reach that they do not help us, but merely lead us to despair. For example, imagine saying to people with defective lives and vile hearts that they should be "pure in heart." One cannot hope to understand, much less live by, the teachings of our Lord until that one has had the spiritual experience with Him that leads one to know Him as Saviour and Lord and Friend. We become changed by Him rather than by His teachings, and the Sermon on the Mount is the pattern of life for those who have received Him as their Saviour.

Here, also, Jesus reveals His method of winning the world: it is through the hearts and the lives of those who have received Him. What faith He had in these disciples to carry His message unto the uttermost parts of the earth! He could see beyond and know that a cross was in His path. He only had to look about Him to see the symbols of the world's power and might. Yet, He intended to win the world with a newness of spirit, with love, and a vision of God as our eternal Father. What optimism He showed when He talked of life's blessedness in the presence of such deep misery among the multitudes He had just seen! Jesus Christ is here revealing His faith in the redemptive power of redeemed lives.

Turn again and read Victor Hugo's *Les Miserables*. We remember how the village was being attacked by robbers who had come down from the mountain to take whatever they could find. The Bishop decided to go out and visit the robbers in their den. People who loved the Bishop so dearly wanted to stop him from going because they knew the robbers would take his life. The Bishop laughed and said that his life on this earth was nothing anyway because he longed to be with Christ. Really, a spirit like that is unconquerable. So, alone he went with faith in the power of Christ to change the hearts of men. We do not know what happened as the Bishop met the robbers. But we do know that the next day the village received back most of the things that had been stolen.

Our Lord understood the power of such a life, and He was saying to those disciples, to those who had committed themselves to Him, "Here is the blueprint, here are the principles, here are the words for changed human lives and the Kingdom of God here on earth."

. . . *and when he was set* [*sat down*] . . .—There is real significance here. In Jesus' day, when a rabbi talked, he always sat down. His official teaching was never done while he was standing or strolling about; it was always

while he was seated. Certainly Matthew understood this
and he was careful to point out that our Lord "sat
down." This is saying that here we have the official words
of the Lord; these are not just offhand comments, but are
basic and eternal principles.

Dr. James T. Fisher, a veteran psychiatrist, made the
following statement: "If you were to take the sum total
of all the authoritative articles ever written by the most
qualified of psychologists and psychiatrists on the subject
of mental hygiene—if you were to combine them and
define them and cleave out the excess verbiage—if you
were to take the whole of the meat and none of the
parsley, and if you were to have these unadulterated bits
of pure scientific knowledge concisely expressed by the
most capable of living poets, you would have an awk-
ward and incomplete summation of the Sermon on the
Mount."

We think of the Sermon on the Mount as the official
summation of the teachings of our Lord. Some feel that
Jesus delivered the Sermon exactly as we have it recorded; others feel that we have recorded an epitome of
all the sermons Jesus ever preached. Whichever, here we
have set down before us the truths of God for the lives
of men.

And he opened his mouth . . .—There is significance in
this phrase. This is much more than merely saying, "He
said." In that day, this expression was used when a very
important utterance was to be given. It gave added meaning and added weight to the words which were to follow.

. . . and taught them . . .—This very statement means
that He had something to say, that He had answers to
life's questions.

Once a father and his young son were driving along

together in a car. The little boy was full of questions. When he saw a train, he asked, "Papa, what makes the train stay on the tracks?"

"I don't know, son."

A short time later the boy saw a boat on the water. He asked, "Papa, what makes a boat stay on top of the water?"

"I do not know, son."

After a time, a plane flew overhead, and the little boy asked, "Papa, what makes an airplane stay in the air?"

"I don't know, son."

The little boy said, "Papa, you don't mind me asking questions, do you?"

"Of course not, son. How are you going to learn, if you never ask any questions?"

The tragedy often is that many teachers have nothing to teach—many preachers have nothing to preach.

Listeners

Another thought—what wonderful listeners those disciples were! We are familiar with the age-old question: If a tree falls in the woods, and there is no ear to hear it, does it make a sound? As far as I know, that question has never been finally settled. But we do know that there can be no teaching if there are none who listen. And how tragic it would have been if those first disciples had not been schooled in the art of listening. For Christ wrote no books; He was dependent upon writing His words upon the hearts of men.

Listening is really a difficult process because the average speaker uses only about a hundred to a hundred and twenty words a minute. But a listener has the ability to hear between three and four hundred words a minute. With the listener's ability to hear being greater than the speaker's to speak, it is quite possible for the mind to slip off into other lines of thought and lose the words of the speaker altogether. It requires real disciplined concentration to hear while another one speaks.

Another stumbling stone to the listener is his own preconceived ideas or prejudices. So often, when a speaker expresses a thought upon which the listener is biased, the listener will automatically turn from the meaning of the speaker to his own point of view.

And, we must remember, there are many ways of listening. One can listen passively; that is, hearing, but paying no attention. Or one may listen partially, failing to hear the whole truth. Or one may listen without being interested, and without response. The disciples so listened as the Master spoke that they not only remembered but gave themselves in complete commitment to what they had heard.

Christian teaching is always far more than a mere giving of information about a way of life. It is dominated by deep concern for the person who is hearing. There is a story that Leonardo da Vinci's career began when his sick teacher asked him to finish a painting which the teacher had begun. Da Vinci protested that he could not do it. The teacher said, "Do your best." Da Vinci did do his best, and when it was finished and the teacher saw it, he exclaimed: "My son, I paint no more." Our Lord wanted to so inspire His earthly disciples that it would not be necessary for Him to be on earth in the flesh any more.

II

II

The Inner Life

OUR LORD BEGINS the Sermon on the Mount by listing the eight qualities of the Christian character. At the very outset, He makes clear the fact that true religion comes from within the heart and the soul of man. Through the years, men have held various ideas of what religion really consists.

(1) For some, religion is knowing the right answers to the right questions, and for them the basis of religious faith is the catechism. Many children have been faithfully taught the questions and answers of the catechism, and their parents and teachers have felt that they were well grounded in the faith. But, as these children mature into adulthood, many times it is tragically evident that their religious faith has no bearing on their lives. It is not enough just to be able to answer questions. Truth must be part of our experience, our emotions, our very inner selves.

(2) Others have felt that the proper religious training began with the memorizing of Bible verses. As children in Sunday school, many of us grew up with the idea that the most important thing we could learn was the memory verse, and that we should be able to quote it at any time. Many people felt that in teaching their children to

· *23*

memorize passages of the Scripture, they were laying the foundations of religious faith. Many of us remember how, as children, we were encouraged to memorize the names of the books of the Bible, and it was a wonderful thing when one could quickly look up a reference in the Bible. We had what we called "Sword Drills," a game in which we chose up sides to see who could find the reference most quickly. Surely no one disputes the value of learning the great language of the Bible, and even knowing how to use the blessed Book; but we have come to the conclusion that unless the Bible is related to life, specifically our own lives, it does not mean its most.

(3) Others have felt that true religion consists of understanding why we act as we act, and the emphasis has been on the study of man, and the problem of evil, as we have emphasized a behavioristic psychology.

(4) Still others have felt that the main concern of religion is the application of its truths to the various social problems of our day. For some, a sermon that does not deal with the race question is not a true gospel sermon. Matters such as war and peace, alcohol, poverty and slums, degrading literature, and all of the other social evils are for many the main concern of religious faith. The purpose of religion, as they see it, is to change all of these evil things.

It Begins Inside

As we begin the Sermon on the Mount, we realize that the main stress in religion is on how to find our true self, and true religious faith begins with the inner man. For many people, religion comes like a Christmas tree. We go out and cut or buy a pretty little tree and bring it into the house. Then we decorate it with lights, and tinsels, and many other things. But all of the beauty comes from what is tacked onto it. On the other hand, consider the apple tree. It is rooted in the soil; it breathes the air; it is warmed by the sunshine and watered by the rain. Life is nurtured inside the tree, and, in due season, blossoms cover the branches, and eventually the fruit comes. As we study the words of Christ, we realize that life begins inside the person and overflows into his attitudes and actions in life.

There is also our tendency to associate God with our surroundings and to feel that God has certain dwelling places. Whenever there is an opportunity, those of us who live in the cities like to get away into the mountains, or to the seashore, or out to the fields. I said to one of the members of my church, "I have been missing you several Sundays now." He said, "Each weekend during this pretty weather, my wife and I have been going out to our cottage in the hill country, which is God's country."

And, in fact, the very first pages of the Bible seem to bear out the idea that God's natural dwelling place is in the country, rather than the city. We read ". . . the Lord God planted a garden . . . in Eden . . ." (GENESIS 2:8). The very first paradise on this earth was a garden that God put here; and we quote the little poem which says:

> One is nearer God's heart in a garden
> Than anywhere else on earth.

> Dorothy Frances Gurney

Read on through the Bible, however, and you come to the next to the last chapter of the Book, in which you read: "And I John saw the holy city, new Jerusalem, coming down from God out of heaven, prepared as a bride adorned for her husband. And I heard a great voice out of heaven saying, Behold, the tabernacle of God is with men, and he will dwell with them, and they shall be his people, and God himself shall be with them, and be their God" (REVELATION 21:2-3). Somehow the dwelling place of God became a city. The first paradise on earth was a garden, and the last paradise a city. The truth is that both are correct: God is in both the countryside and the city. The important thing is not where we are, but what we are inside. It is the inner man that counts, rather than his surroundings; the transformation comes from within. Wherever we are called to live—on hillside or valley, in suburb or city apartment—the light of Christ within the soul can make a paradise out of that place.

The Beatitudes

Blessed are the poor in spirit: for theirs is the kingdom of heaven.

Blessed are they that mourn: for they shall be comforted.

Blessed are the meek: for they shall inherit the earth.

Blessed are they which do hunger and thirst after righteousness: for they shall be filled.

Blessed are the merciful: for they shall obtain mercy.

Blessed are the pure in heart: for they shall see God.

Blessed are the peacemakers: for they shall be called the children of God.

Blessed are they which are persecuted for righteousness' sake: for theirs is the kingdom of heaven.

Blessed are ye, when men shall revile you, and persecute you, and shall say all manner of evil against you falsely, for my sake.

Rejoice, and be exceeding glad: for great is your re-
ward in heaven: for so persecuted they the prophets
which were before you (MATTHEW 5:3-12).

The word we begin with is "blessed." Some have objected to the word "blessed" and have re-translated it
"happy." "Blessed" is really much better, and a stronger
word. The Greek word is *makarios,* which is a word used
to describe the gods. The word "blessed" literally means:
an inner joy that is untouchable by the world. The word
"happiness" is built on the word "hap," and literally
means: chance. Human happiness is often dependent on
the chances of life, over which so often man has no control. A sudden illness, a deep disappointment, the loss of
some material blessing—one of many things can change
happiness into sorrow. But when the Christian has God
within his soul, nothing on earth can touch him. In the
Sermon on the Mount, Christ points to the eight qualities
of character which bring blessedness to the human life—
a permanent joy. It is the same blessedness which He
later refers to when He says, "Peace I leave with you,
my peace I give unto you: not as the world giveth, give I
unto you. Let not your heart be troubled, neither let it
be afraid" (JOHN 14:27).

Right at this point, we are more apt to miss the real
purpose of the Christian faith. We talk so much about
sacrifice, service, and the will of God that leads to a
cross. We miss the truth that Christ's purpose is to make
men happy; His typical greeting was: "Be of good
cheer." In fact, it has been pointed out that He gave the
world "three cheers." First, the cheer of forgiveness: He
said, ". . . be of good cheer; thy sins be forgiven thee"
(MATTHEW 9:2). Second, the cheer of companionship:
He said, "Be of good cheer; it is I; be not afraid" (MAT-
THEW 14:27). Third, the cheer of victory: He said, "In

the world ye shall have tribulation; but be of good cheer; I have overcome the world" (JOHN 16:33). What are the three things that destroy blessedness? A sense of guilt; a feeling of forsakenness; a fear of defeat. "Three cheers," said Christ; "I bring you the answer to all three."

So, at the beginning of the Sermon, Jesus gives the eight qualities of life that result in true happiness. Just as an octave in music contains eight notes, so there are eight notes that make up the melody of the Christian life. We call them the Beatitudes.

If you named the conditions under which life would be best for you, would you name these eight: poor in spirit, mourn, meek, hunger and thirst, merciful, pure in heart, peacemakers, and persecuted? If you possessed those eight things in your life, would they make you a blessed person? Jesus thought so.

Before you say He is wrong, set those qualities against their opposites, as is suggested in *The Interpreter's Bible*. The opposite of poor in spirit is proud in spirit. The opposite of mourn is being light-headed, not caring, pleasure-seeking. The opposite of the meek are the aggressors. The opposite of the persecuted are those who play it safe, who compromise, who never take a stand for the right.

Jesus told of two men who went to pray. Which found the greater happiness? The one who prayed, "God, I thank thee, that I am not as other men are . . . ," or the one who prayed, "God be merciful to me a sinner" (LUKE 18:11, 13)? One was proud; the other was poor. Which was the blessed?

Consider Christ and Hitler. One said, "I am meek and lowly in heart . . ." (MATTHEW 11:29). The other said, "I shall conquer and rule the world." Which of the two found real happiness?

Look at Simon Peter. At one moment in his life he was cursing and denying that he ever knew Christ; at another moment he was being crucified for preaching Christ. In which moment was he happier?

We Americans have more to make life easy than any people who have ever lived. We live in the finest houses, wear the nicest clothes, and eat the best food that any generation has ever known; yet, at the same time, today we have more suicides, more divorces, more people in jail, more mental illnesses than any people of all time. For many people, life is a grim, desperate, unhappy affair. We would do well to begin living by the eight principles Christ said would make us happy.

Poor in spirit—not satisfied with ourselves, but ever looking upward.

Mourn—a heart that never feels sorrow will never feel joy. Through grief we grow strong as we let God into our hearts through the broken places.

Meek—we neither rebel against life nor submit to our misfortunes. Rather, we accept life as it is, and we cooperate with the will and plan of God.

Hunger and thirst after righteousness—our greatest ambition is not how much we can possess, but how right our lives can become.

Merciful—we keep clean of grudges and the poisons of hate, anger, jealousy, and bitterness. Mercy overlooks the little things and forgives the large things.

Pure in heart—we set a worthy goal for our lives. As we become attached to some high purpose, and give ourselves to it, we do find God.

Peacemakers—there are so many occasions to give ourselves to the ministry of God's peace.

Persecuted for righteousness' sake—the high purpose

of our lives lifts above the pain and those who would hurt and harm us.

These, said Jesus, are the steps to happiness—to more than mere happiness: to blessedness!

In the days of the Spanish Inquisition, every kind of terrible torture that men could devise was used. The tormentors found that the very worst punishment was to put a man into a cell where the ceiling was not high enough for him to stand at his full height. He was never able to stand straight, to hold up his head. This, it was discovered, would break a man's spirit quicker than any other punishment.

Read again the Beatitudes. They are saying, "Stand up straight; be a real person."

The Salt of the Earth

Ye are the salt of the earth: but if the salt have lost his savour, wherewith shall it be salted? it is thenceforth good for nothing, but to be cast out, and to be trodden under foot of men (MATTHEW 5:13).

Here our Lord is saying that one who is a Christian is not only good, but good for something; and, in using the analogy of salt, He is using one of the strongest words He could have used. In His day, and indeed in this day, salt is one of the most precious items of mankind. It is told that, many centuries ago, the Chinese had a terrible way of killing their enemies. They would give them all the food they wanted, but would first remove the salt from that food. Slowly but surely these people died because their bodies could not exist without salt. Visit the hospitals today, and you will see patients being given a saline solution which helps to keep life in their bodies.

(1) Salt has always been known as one of the finest preservatives that mankind has. Before the days of modern refrigeration, the farmer would kill his hog and salt it down to preserve the meat. Likewise, salt preserves society itself. Just as a human being does not naturally grow good, neither does society. Society tends toward rottenness and decay.

One of the most thrilling stories in all of the Bible was that of Elijah being carried to heaven in the chariot of fire. Elisha, the younger prophet, watched the great man ascending, and shouted, "My father, my father, the chariot of Israel, and the horsemen thereof" (II KINGS 2:12). He was saying that the man going yonder, who had gone about calling people to God, was really the defender of his nation. I am sure there were many then who felt that the defense of Israel was in her chariots and horsemen, her armor, her battleships, and her warriors. But one with deeper insight could see that the real defense of any nation lay in the character of her people.

Study the history of the civilizations of the world, and you will see that not one has ever been destroyed by outside forces. Civilization decays from within.

(2) We remind ourselves that salt gives flavor to everything it touches. Without salt, many foods are tasteless and even sickening. For many people, the Christian life appears to be an insipid affair. How many people have turned away from the faith with the idea: "I want to have a good time"; and, then, in later years, they learn the truth that it isn't religion that puts premature gray hairs on a head, and pain in a heart, and a body in a premature grave! The true faith gives brightness and joy to life.

Here is a warning for many who now claim to be Christians. Oliver Wendell Holmes is quoted as saying, "I might have entered the ministry if certain clergymen I knew had not looked and acted so much like undertakers." For too many people, the Christian life has been a dull affair concerned mainly with prohibitions.

In recent years we have witnessed a change in the services of many of the churches in this country. I am not sure that the change is altogether good. We used to have our revivals, when people would come together with great enthusiasm. We would sing the so-called gospel songs which stirred up our emotions. Under the power of great preaching, many times people were even moved to express their feelings with shouting. In some cases, believers even went to extreme forms of expression, such as "holy-rolling." Great numbers of people came and wept at the altar. Gradually, we introduced into our churches much more formal services. Many times the beauty of the Lord is expressed through formal and aesthetic worship services. But there is a danger of our services becoming so formal that they become dead. I have known people who go to a football or a baseball game, and in the moment of excitement stand on their seats and shout at the top of their lungs. Yet those same people would be deeply incensed at an outward expression of one's feeling in the worship of God. Frankly, I would rather try to restrain a fanatic than resurrect a corpse. I am not appealing for mere emotionalism in our faith, but I am appealing that the emotion not be eliminated. The Christian faith is not merely a matter of the mind; it certainly also is an experience of the heart and the feelings.

(3) Salt makes its presence known. . . . *if the salt have lost his savour* [*taste*]. . . . Some chemists have ob-

jected to this statement because they say it is an impossibility: salt is chloride of sodium, and, as long as it lasts, it is salt and nothing but salt. But Jesus was not speaking as a scientist or a chemist; He was talking about the ordinary ways of men. What He was saying was that when a person ceases to really be the person he claims to be, then he is "good for nothing."

Many of us remember with delight and joy the old home-made ice cream. In freezing the ice cream, it was necessary to use salt with the ice. Some of us painfully remember occasions when we opened the top of the freezer to see if the cream had frozen, and maybe to sample it a bit, and inadvertently let a little of the salt water into the ice cream. Then, when the cream was served at dinner, you could taste the salt very plainly. The point is: salt makes itself known.

Once there was a young man, a Christian, who went to work a summer in a lumber camp. Some of his friends told him that those rough lumbermen would make life miserable for him because of his religious faith. Bravely he went and spent the summer. When he came home, his friends asked how he made out. "Did they laugh at your being a Christian?" He said, "No, they did not laugh at me because of my being a Christian. They never did find it out."

There are those who say that we should never discuss two subjects with our friends: politics and religion. But one of our hymns states, "What we have seen and heard, with confidence we tell." The Christian has to let it be known. It was the Psalmist who said, "Let the redeemed of the Lord say so . . ." (PSALM 107:2).

(4) Let us remember that Jesus said, "Ye are the salt of the earth. . . ." He did not say, "Ye are the salt of *heaven*." Through the ages, some have been tempted to

leave this evil world and be alone with the Lord. The ascetic life has much appeal to many people—so much appeal, that down through the centuries many people have withdrawn into isolation. Many of us have felt what the Psalmist felt when he said, "oh that I had wings like a dove! for then would I fly away, and be at rest" (PSALM 55:6). Even one of the greatest of the prophets on one occasion said, "Oh that I had in the wilderness a lodging place of wayfaring men; that I might leave my people, and go from them!" (JEREMIAH 9:2). But a Christian cannot and does not run away. The Christian lives in his world, is a part of it, and makes his presence and influence felt in every possible way.

(5) Another thought: look at salt through a microscope, and you see immediately that it is not a mass of something, but, rather, is made up of many individual grains. Some grains of salt are large, some small, and they come in all different shapes. Does not that indicate something to us? The salt of the earth, as Jesus was thinking of it, is not one great mass. Christianity is made up of many individuals of all shapes and sizes, and, like the salt of the earth, we do not lose our individuality. One may preach, one may sing, one may give large gifts. There are many, many contributions to make, and no one of us can make all of the contributions; but, as individuals, each one of us gives some contribution, and all together we become truly the salt of the earth, in His name.

In Lloyd C. Douglas' *The Big Fisherman*, we read these arresting words: "He didn't talk in a loud voice; not like a teacher or a preacher. . . . The carpenter didn't seem to be speaking to the crowd—as a crowd, but to each person, as if they were alone together, apart. . . . That was the first thing I noticed about His talk. I couldn't help feeling that He had singled me out and was speaking directly to me. Maybe that was why I wanted to get closer. I suppose that was why everyone crowded in; wanting to get closer." As Jesus thinks of us, He thinks of us as persons, one by one.

In *The Confidential Clerk*, T. S. Eliot had Lady Elizabeth say it this way: "Of course, there is something in us, in all of us, which isn't just heredity, but something unique, something we have been from eternity. Something . . . straight from God." It is that "something unique" which Jesus always sees in a person.

Or, maybe Doctor Zhivago said it better in these words: "When the gospel says that in the Kingdom of God there are neither Jews nor Gentiles, does it merely mean that all are equal in the sight of God? No—the gospel wasn't needed for that. The Greek philosophers, the Roman moralists, and the Hebrew prophets had known this long before, but it said: In that new way of living and new form of society, which is born of the heart, and which is called the Kingdom of Heaven, there are no nations, there are only individuals."

(6) Very familiar has become the slogan of one of the salt companies, "When it rains, it pours." Because salt gathers moisture, it is necessary that an ingredient be added to it; this ingredient, sodium carbonate, when added to the salt, wraps each individual grain in something like a little protective package. It serves to keep out the moisture and enables the salt always to pour, no matter how hard the rain. Does not this have something to say to the Christian? When the Christian life is wrapped by the grace of God, it is able to keep on going in any and every circumstance. In this sense, the Christian is sheltered and undergirded and surrounded and protected.

(7) Let us note that our Lord did not say, "You are the *sugar* of the earth." Many times we think of the

Christian life as something so gentle and meek and mild as to be almost meaningless. The Christian is a powerful force and influence in his world. When salt gets into a wound, it stings and hurts; and when God's children are among those who are wrong toward God, their presence stings and hurts and is felt. Sin might be thought of as an open wound, and salt gives it annoyance and distress that makes it very uncomfortable. Truly, the Christian can be an irritating force in his society.

In ancient Palestine, the fuel for cooking purposes was very poor. The people there would put plates of salt in their stoves, next to the fire, which would add noticeably to the heat of the flame. Does not this suggest something of the life of the Christian? As we lay our lives beside our Lord's life, His work becomes stronger and more effective in this world.

The Light of the World

Ye are the light of the world. A city that is set on an hill cannot be hid.

Neither do men light a candle, and put it under a bushel, but on a candlestick; and it giveth light unto all that are in the house.

Let your light so shine before men, that they may see your good works, and glorify your Father which is in heaven (MATTHEW 5:14-16).

(1) First, let us remind ourselves that light is something; darkness is nothing. Light is positive; darkness is negative. So many times we get the idea that religion consists only of prohibitions, and that one becomes a Christian by not doing certain things that he feels are

wrong. Actually, the Christian faith leads one into life rather than away from life. One night, when Robert Louis Stevenson was a child six or seven years old, he was at the window watching the lamplighter at work. One by one, the lighter would light the lamps as he walked down the street. Young Stevenson was fascinated and silent. His nurse feared that his quietness meant he was up to some mischief. She called out, asking what he was doing. The little child answered, "I am watching a man making holes in the darkness." Later he wrote a lovely little poem depicting his experience, which is included in *A Child's Garden of Verses*. There you have the Christian life: "Making holes in the darkness."

Every so often some person says to me, "I want you to give me some church work to do." What he means is some job in the church—maybe playing the piano, or singing in the choir, helping in the kitchen, being an usher, doing part-time secretarial work, being made an officer of a Sunday school class, or being named to the official board of the church. All of these things are important in the life of the church, and must be done, but let us remember that these things are not really church work. The true work of the church is done through Christian lives revealing Christ in everyday work and play, and at home. The church work that counts for the most is being a Christian wherever we are, all of the time.

I love the institution of the church, and give myself to it. But sometimes I feel that in the church we give too much attention to things that do not matter, and do not meet the needs of people. In his book *If Winter Comes*, A. S. M. Hutchinson has one of his characters (Mark Sabre) say a wonderful thing: "I tell you, Hapgood, that plumb down in the crypt and abyss of every man's soul is a hunger, a craving for other food than this earthly stuff. And the churches know it; and instead of reaching down to him what he wants—light—instead of that, they invite him to dancing and picture-shows, and you're a jolly good fellow, and religion's a jolly fine thing and no spoilsport, and all that sort of latter-day tendency. . . . He can get all that outside the churches and get it better. Light, light! He wants light, Hapgood, and the padres come down and drink beer with him, and watch boxing matches with him, and sing music-hall songs with him, and dance jazz with him, and call it making religion a Living Thing in the Lives of the People. Lift the hearts of the people to God, they say, by showing them that religion is not incompatible with having a jolly fine time. And there's no God there that a man can understand for him to be lifted up to. Hapgood, a man wouldn't care what he had to give up, if he knew he was making for something inestimably precious. But he doesn't know. Light, light—that's what he wants; and the longer it's withheld, the lower he'll sink."

What an indictment against many of us in the church! The church has Christ to offer, and Christ is positive and real.

(2) In the second place, light is to be seen. "Neither do men light a candle, and put it under a bushel, but on a candlestick. . . ." Let us remember that, in Jesus' day, people did not have matches, as we have today. Thus, it was not easy to relight a lamp. So, when they were going out of the house for a time, for fear the opening and closing of the door would blow the light out, and for safety's sake, they took the lamp down from its stand and put it under a bushel measure where it could burn without the danger of its being blown out. Of course, as long as the light was under this large container, it could give

no light to the house. Jesus' disciples understood fully what He meant about putting their light "under a bushel."

Christianity is something to be seen. It is not something to be kept a secret; and not only is it to be seen within the fellowship, but in the entire world—"Ye are the light of the *world*." We speak often of hypocrites, and certainly we do not mean it as a complimentary term. Normally, we think of a hypocrite as one who appears to be better than he really is. But there is another side to the coin: a hypocrite may be one who fails to appear as good as he really is. One can be a hypocrite by being ashamed of his convictions, by failing to uphold the faith, by refusing to speak out at the proper time. One may hide his light under a bushel of cowardice, of prejudice, or of temper. One's light might be snuffed out by some positive wrong.

The burning candle has become one of the symbols of the Christian faith. And one thing you notice about it is that the candle burns most beautifully when it stands upright. The Christian whose life is upright in thought and action will become an illuminating witness in a dark and sinful world.

St. Paul warns us to "Abstain from all appearance of evil" (I THESSALONIANS 5:22). How often it is that the light of a Christian life is snuffed out because of some questionable action, or perhaps even the appearance of some questionable action. Conversely, the Christian is commanded not only to be good, but to give the appearance of goodness. He must not only love Christ in his heart, but let his life reveal that fact.

(3) One of the qualities of light is that it cannot be soiled. Your hands may be covered with dirt, but when you grasp a beam of light, you leave no mark of that dirt

upon it. You may shine a beam into the worst filth, but none of it will stick to the light. So—one who is the light will not be soiled in any circumstance or situation.

(4) Light is one of the most cheerful and cheering things this world knows. Admiral Robert E. Peary discovered the North Pole; telling about the long journey there, he said that the greatest obstacle to be overcome in the Arctic was not the cold, but the long darkness. The continual absence of light took away the spirit of the men. One of the worst punishments you could inflict upon any person would be to cause him to stay in absolute darkness for an extended period of time.

I once had my study just off the sanctuary in a church. It was sometimes my habit to work late into the night in my study, but many nights I found it a distracting experience. The large sanctuary was dark, and I would hear all manner of noises as I tried to work. I would imagine a thief was breaking in, and it was quite disconcerting. Yet I could work in the same study in the daytime, and those noises never bothered me.

Every physician knows that people can be in pain during the day and bear it; but, as the darkness comes and as the night moves on, the pain becomes unbearable to the point where they can stand it no longer. Physicians understand why many people phone for help at night when they might have phoned during the day.

(5) Another thing about light is that it reveals the way; it is a guide. Man has five physical senses, and through each of these five senses man learns. Yet it is through the sense of sight that man learns the most.

Someone conducted an experiment with a group of people; the object was to test their powers of observation. The people were brought into a room and kept there for a period of time. Then they were brought out again and asked to make a list of the things in the room. Nearly every list dealt exclusively with items the people saw with their eyes. There were many other things in the room, such as the fragrance of flowers, the sound of music, the warmth from a heater, and the softness of the chairs. But the people were impressed more by what they saw than by what they smelled or heard or felt. Truly it is seeing that is our main source of knowledge; and it is because of light that we can see.

Why have multitudes across the centuries followed Christ? Is it because of what He said? Certainly we cherish His words, but if His words were all we had to go by, would there really be any followers? No. We follow *Him*. It is seeing His light that has the deepest influence upon each of us and upon our world.

When I started out in the ministry, I felt that the most important thing was preparing sermons. Sermons are important, but not most important. I was pastor of one church for twelve years, and during those years I preached more than a thousand sermons in that church. Were I to go back today and ask the people of that church, "Tell me the sermons that I preached here in this church," I daresay that many of them would be hard-pressed to name even as few as ten of those sermons. But, on the other hand, all the people of that church would be able to tell me about how I lived, the spirit I had, the impression my life made. I now have come to realize that the minister brings the greatest light by the life he lives, rather than by the words he speaks. One is reminded of the old saying: "What you are speaks so loudly I cannot hear what you say."

Thus, Jesus did not say we are to bring the light; He said we *are* the light. It is not by words, nor by actions, but by our very being that we represent Him who is the true Light. A lovely flower and an ugly weed are really the same in the darkness. It is only when the light is thrown upon them that their difference is known. And it is only in the light that we see the difference between a life lived with God and a life lived without God. It is only in the light that we see ourselves—our failures and mistakes—and our great possibilities.

(6) Light makes shadows. In his play *Macbeth*, Shakespeare wrote this line, "Life's but a walking shadow. . . ." Sometimes we are almost overwhelmed by the deep shadows which fall across our world and our lives. We become discouraged as we see the plagues of vice and crime over our world, the horror of war, discrimination against people, the low state of morals, and all the other shadows. But let us remember that shadows are created by light, and if there were no light, then there would be no shadows. The fact that we see shadows in our world is evidence of the existence of light, and thus the shadows become a source of encouragement and strength. The brighter the light, the deeper the shadows.

There is an inscription on the wall of a castle in Scotland which reads: "When Jesus comes, the shadows depart." Such is not the case. The truth is: when Jesus comes, the shadows develop, because without the Light, there would be no shadows.

At various times, in parts of the world, people have taken for granted such things as illness, ignorance, bondage of women, exploiting of children, deplorable prison conditions, slavery, war, superstition; and the list goes on and on. These things have been accepted as normal parts of life until the light of Christ has been thrown upon them; then these very things have become dark and ugly shadows about which men have felt compelled to do something. Not all of the problems of the world have been solved, but the process is now going on.

When asked how he discovered the law of gravity, Sir Isaac Newton replied, "By thinking about it continuously. I keep the object of my research constantly before me, waiting until the first light begins to dawn. Little by little, finally, this changes, and at last the light is complete." The Christian deals with all the evils of the world in the same way, and he has faith to believe that someday the light will be complete in the solving of all of the problems of mankind.

(7) Another thing about light is that, in order to be light, it must be consumed. A candle cannot give light without, at the same time, giving itself. Thus, to be light is a very costly process. The Christian not only gives of his time, of his money, of his energies, of his talent—the Christian gives of himself, and is willing to be consumed. The story of the faith is still with those who died that Christ might live.

In his book *The Silver Chalice*, Thomas B. Costain gives us real insight. One of the characters, Basil, had difficulty finding a response that would convey the truest clue to the state of his mind. "I believe in Jesus," he said. "I believe Him to be the Son of the One and Only God. I believe He will return to this earth, and I hope His coming will not be long delayed, but because I do not share the ecstasy which these beliefs have brought to others, I think there must be a vital point of conviction that I have not reached."

Cephas, another character, nodded his head. "Some time soon it will come. It may be that you will suffer a severe blow or that you will be called upon to make a sacrifice. In the strain of such a moment your eyes will be opened. The tinder in your heart will take fire. You will feel a great happiness gain possession of you. The world will light up, and the sun will shine in all the dark places where before you saw nothing but shadows. You will cry out what you believe, and you will want everyone to hear."

Truly it is, that in the moment of some great sacrifice we really become the brightest light.

(7) Each individual light is important. Let us close this discussion of light with something out of the imagination of Dr. Paul W. Quillian, one of the greatest ministers this nation of ours has ever produced:

"I don't make any difference," said a ray of light, as it left the sun on its journey earthward. "I am going to go where I please and do what I please. There are so many other rays that I will never be missed."

"I'll go with you," said a second ray.

"So will I," said a third. "What about our duty, you say? Why that's an old-fashioned word that has lost its meaning. We're free to do as we please."

And so, where a moment ago there had been three brilliant rays of light plunging earthward, there were now three momentary blurs, three tiny absences of light.

Down on earth a young man is purchasing an engagement ring for his sweetheart. He wants a perfect stone without a single flaw to symbolize their plighted troth. He takes the stone he has almost decided upon and carries it to the open door. There in the bright sunshine he peers through the jeweler's magnifying glass, searching for a hidden flaw. Now, there is a flaw in this stone. Will he see it? Yes, the light is brilliant. But wait—just as his eye is about to detect the flaw, a strange blur comes over his vision. There is a tiny absence of light as his eye passes over the flaw. The failure of the first ray has resulted in a lover's deception.

The scene changes, and we see into the room of a farm home where a surgeon is operating on the eye of a child. It is an emergency operation. No hospital facilities are near enough to be used, and so the surgeon has placed his unconscious little patient near the window where the bright sunlight pouring through can be reflected from the mirror on his forehead and deep into the eye socket where his skilled fingers are deftly at work. One by one the arteries have been tied, the nerves and muscles pushed aside with care. He is ready for the last delicate stroke of the lancet when suddenly the light becomes blurred, his knife goes too deep. The failure of the second ray has cost a child the gift of sight.

Once more the scene is changed. We see two young aviators piloting a fighter plane across the Atlantic. For hours they have been flying in a dense fog. They have lost their bearings. The plane had evidently been too hastily inspected before they took off, and hours earlier they had learned that their instruments could not be relied upon. Anxiously, the navigator looks for a break in the fog. Just one glimpse of the sun and time to take a reading on his instrument, and they would have their bearings. At last there is a rift in the fog; the sun breaks through. Eagerly, the navigator snatches up his instruments; hastily, he makes the adjustments; now for the reading! But he canot see—there is a momentary blur. The sun is gone behind the fog once more, and the failure of the third ray has cost two boys their lives.

How queer to end a sermon with an imaginary story like that, someone is saying. But are these stories imaginary?

I know two lovers who, because a Christian failed to let his light shine when it was needed, have plighted their troth with a fatal flaw in it.

I know a child who, because a Christian father failed to let his light shine, will go spiritually blinded through life.

I know two boys who, because a Christian failed to let his light shine at a time he thought made no difference, have been lost in the sea of life.

Yes, you are important, very important, you who love Christ. Jesus said: "Ye are the light of the world."

III

III

The Law
and the Spirit

*Think not that I am come to destroy the law, or the
prophets: I am not come to destroy, but to fulfil.*

*For verily I say unto you, Till heaven and earth pass,
one jot or one tittle shall in no wise pass from the law, till
all be fulfilled.*

*Whosoever therefore shall break one of these least
commandments, and shall teach men so, he shall be called
the least in the kingdom of heaven: but whosoever shall
do and teach them, the same shall be called great in the
kingdom of heaven* (MATTHEW 5:17-19).

When Jesus brought up the matter of the Law, I am
sure the interest of His disciples was immediately height-
ened, for two reasons: (1) the Law was something they
were constantly faced with. In that day the Jewish Law
contained some 613 commandments. Today there are
those in the church who would have difficulty naming
even the Ten Commandments. Think how it would be if
we had 613 laws with which to deal! (2) In the second
place, Jesus had already become known as a law-breaker,
and we may be sure these disciples wanted to see how He
would defend Himself.

As you read the gospels, you find many occasions when it seems that He completely disregarded the established laws of that day, such as healing people and plucking corn on the sabbath. Surely He must have disregarded numerous of the Jewish laws of which we have no record. Perhaps the disciples felt that He would denounce the laws of that day, but He surprised them. He said, *I am not come to destroy, but to fulfil*. He announced that He did not want one jot or tittle to pass from the Law. A jot in that day was somewhat like an apostrophe in our language today; a tittle was the little line projecting from the bottom of a letter. For Jesus the Law was so sacred that even the smallest part of it must be eternal.

Constructive Positiveness

To begin with, He gave the Law a constructive positiveness by reminding the people that the Law really was. Look ahead in the Gospel of Matthew to chapter 22, where it is recorded that a lawyer asked Jesus a question, saying, "Master, which is the greatest commandment in the law?" In answer to that question, Jesus quoted from chapter 16 of Deuteronomy and chapter 19 of Leviticus: "Thou shalt love the Lord thy God with all thy heart, and with all thy soul, and with all thy mind. This is the first and great commandment. And the second is like unto it, Thou shalt love thy neighbour as thyself. On these two commandments hang all the law and the prophets" (MATTHEW 22:36-40). Here you see the predominant thought is not *thou shalt not*; rather is the Law to be predominated by compelling *thou shalts*. Many of the laws of the scribes and the Pharisees were mere prohibitions. Now, I know there are many things we should not do. However, no amount of the things we do not do add up to being a Christian.

The other day I saw an old-fashioned wooden Indian standing out in front of a store in a city I was visiting. Suppose I had stopped and visited with that gentleman, and suppose I had been of a mind to put temptation before him? I might have said, "I know how we can make some easy money. It is a bit dishonest, but we can get by with it." Or I might have said, "I know where we can buy some cheap bootleg liquor out of which we can make a good profit." Or I might have said, "I know where there's a bank that would be real easy to rob, if you would help me." In fact, I might have listed a hundred things that were wrong and sought to tempt him with them; yet to none of them my friend the wooden Indian would have responded.

I might have decided, "Well, here is a good man." And I might have been encouraged to invite him to go with me to church. I might have suggested some needy person in the community he could help. I might have suggested some worthy cause that needed a leader. I might have suggested a man who needed someone to speak to him about the Christ and the Christian Way. I might have named many good works that he might do, and yet to those suggestions I would have received the same lack of response.

Even though that wooden Indian committed absolutely nothing wrong, still he could not be counted as a Christian. A lot of the people in Jesus' day had progressed in their religious faith and life to the point where that wooden Indian had progressed.

The Spirit Versus Authority

The basic difference between Jesus and the Pharisees was this: He preached a religion of the spirit, and they insisted on a religion of authority. Religion of authority has all of the answers in black and white—everything is put down, and one needs only to grasp it and obey it. Everything is already decided.

The other day I took a trip with a friend of mine on his boat. We went far out into the Gulf of Mexico. Do you think my friend had to sit up and hold the wheel and watch the compass all the time? No. He had an automatic pilot on that boat; all he had to do was set the course, and automatically the boat was kept on that course. So it is with the religion of authority. You can never change your course, it is all set. Everything is worked out. You do not even dare to pose a question. Your only task is to bring your life under sufficient discipline.

John Henry Newman changed from a religion of the spirit to a religion of authority. Later, he wrote in his spiritual diary these words: "All doubt and adventure for me have come to an end." He was right. In accepting complete authority over his life, he did rid himself of all doubt, but he had insight to see that he also lost all the opportunity and spirit of adventure.

Ernest Fremont Tittle put it this way: "Religions of authority in some form will not only survive, but they will flourish as long as there are people who would rather feel certain than find truth." Religions of authority offer only dead answers out of a dead past for a deadly existence.

On the other hand, the religion of the spirit offers a

chance for an abundant, full and joyful life. St. Augustine summed it all up when he said, "Love God, and do as you please." Surely we know the great saint was not saying that we have license to do any and every thing. He had enough understanding to know that when one's affection is firmly fixed on God, his actions will turn out right. For such a one, the adventurous life goes far beyond the law. The English preacher, Dick Shepherd, said that being a Christian does not consist in refraining from doing things which no gentlemen would think of doing anyway, but in doing good things which a mere gentleman would not think of doing.

The Christian recognizes the necessity of the law. For example, he drives down a city street, and there are laws as to how fast he should drive; there are traffic lights at each corner. It would be foolish to trust a city's traffic to the mere loving of our neighbors. However, the Christian recognizes the reason for regulations, and obeys them, not from force, but from the impulse of the heart.

For an illustration, look at the difference in a couple when they are courting and when they are in court. When they are courting, the thing each is thinking about is how much he can do to please the other, and how happy he can make the other. But, after a couple have married, and the marriage has broken up, and they find themselves in court, frequently each is trying to see how little he can get by with doing for the other; sometimes it seems that each is trying to see how miserable he can make the other. Yes, there is a vast difference in our actions when we are dealing under the impulse of love and under the regulation of the law.

The Pharisees' Righteousness

For I say unto you, That except your righteousness shall exceed the righteousness of the scribes and Pharisees, ye shall in no case enter into the kingdom of heaven (MATTHEW 5:20).

Did Jesus mean that we are to live more righteously than the Pharisees? If He did, He was giving us a large order, because they were indeed righteous people. They were active church members and regular in their attendance; they gave a tithe of their income; they carefully obeyed every detail of the law. Really, the Pharisees were people who conscientiously did right. But go back to the illustration of the difference between the Christmas tree and the apple tree. The Pharisees sought to put on their goodness from the outside, while the Christian nurtures the inner life and the actions naturally take care of themselves. Both the Pharisees and the Christians obey the law, but they come at it from different directions, with different motives. In truth, the way the Pharisees select is an impossible way. Who can even know, much less keep, all of the laws? But when the heart is right, then the task becomes much easier and much more within reach.

Thou Shalt Not Kill

Now our Lord illustrates this truth with specific examples:

Ye have heard that it was said by them of old time,

Thou shalt not kill; and whosoever shall kill shall be in danger of the judgment:

But I say unto you, That whosoever is angry with his brother without a cause shall be in danger of the judgment: and whosoever shall say to his brother, Raca, shall be in danger of the council: but whosoever shall say, Thou fool, shall be in danger of hell fire.

Therefore if thou bring thy gift to the altar, and there rememberest that thy brother hath ought against thee;

Leave there thy gift before the altar, and go thy way; first be reconciled to thy brother, and then come and offer thy gift.

Agree with thine adversary quickly, whiles thou art in the way with him; lest at any time the adversary deliver thee to the judge, and the judge deliver thee to the officer, and thou be cast into prison.

Verily I say unto thee, Thou shalt by no means come out thence, till thou hast paid the uttermost farthing (MATTHEW 5:21-26).

Jesus begins with the sacredness of human life: "Thou shalt not kill . . ."; but rather than deal merely with the deed of murder, He goes to the very cause of murder, which is anger and lack of respect for another human being. *"But I say unto you, That whosoever is angry with his brother without a cause . . ."*—in the *Revised Standard Version of the Bible,* the words "without cause" are omitted because in the best manuscripts that phrase was not contained. Our Lord is really saying that there is no reason and no circumstance under which I am permitted to be angry with my fellow man.

In this connection, one immediately remembers the time when our Lord Himself went into the temple where there was a man whose hand was withered. It is recorded,

· 55

". . . when he had looked round about on them with anger . . ." (MARK 3:5). There are other instances when Jesus expressed the emotion of anger, and we recall that St. Paul said, "Be ye angry, and sin not . . ." (EPHESIANS 4:26). Anger is certainly not always condemned in the Bible. God gave to His people the ability to feel anger, and He expected it to be used; in fact, there are times when it is a sin not to be angry. Evil abounds in our world because Christian people refuse to get angry about it. Wrong must be driven out by angry Christians, just as, when Jesus walked into the temple and saw it being desecrated by money-changers, He took a whip and drove them out. Tolerance of evil may be worse than the evil itself.

In his book *Two Friends of Man*, Ralph Coingold quotes one as saying, "Hull, do try to moderate your indignation, and keep more cool; why, you are all on fire."

His friend replied, "Brother May, I have need to be all on fire, for I have mountains of ice about me to melt."

The evil and wrong in our world will never be destroyed or driven out until good people are aroused enough to do something about it. Truly, there are times to become righteously indignant.

But notice carefully that, in this passage, Jesus is not talking about situations; He is talking about people, and He is saying that we must not be angry with another person. We all know how others can, in various ways, irritate us and upset us, but when we have this Spirit of Christ within our hearts we become more immune to irritations. We are able to bear so much more.

Charles L. Wallis tells of a Hindu woman who was suffering great persecution from her husband at the time she was converted. When the missionary asked her what she did when her husband became angry, the woman said, "Well, sir, I cook his food better; when he complains, I sweep the floor cleaner; and when he speaks unkindly, I answer him mildly. I try, sir, to show him that when I became a Christian, I became a better wife and a better mother."

With the Spirit of Christ inside our hearts, we are able to overcome the irritations that used to cause us to lose our tempers and become angry. In the long ago, the scholar Plutarch said, "I learned that anger is not incurable if one wants to cure it." Sometimes one says, "I have a temper," as if that were something to brag about. The truth is, every person has a temper, and I have suggested that there is a time and a place to use it. But there is never a time for our temper to get out of control with out fellow man.

In Jesus' day, each local community had a judgment court before which one could be carried for the crime of anger, and this is what He was referring to when He said that whoever is angry with his brother *shall be in danger of the judgment*. . . .

Then, our Lord goes further and uses the word *Raca*. Those who gave us the *King James Version of the Bible* made no attempt to translate this word. The *Revised Standard Version* translates it: ". . . whoever insults his brother. . . ." Actually, this means "to hold one in contempt, to look down upon, to hold a snobbish attitude." Positively, it means that every human being is a creature of God, and, as such, is to be looked upon with respect and appreciation. One of the most glorious things about this land of America is expressed by Thomas Wolfe in his book *You Can't Go Home Again*. He said, "To every man, his chance—to every man, regardless of his birth, his shining, golden opportunity—to every man the right to live, to work, to be himself, and to become whatever thing his manhood and his vision can combine to make him—this, seeker, is the promise of America." For me to look down upon any person because of his parentage, or his labor, is a sin. Snobbery which comes from pride of birth or opportunity is one of the ugliest things in humanity. One guilty of this, said Jesus, . . . *shall be in danger of the council* . . . ; that is, the judgment of the Sanhedrin.

Then Jesus goes on to say, . . . *whosoever shall say, Thou fool, shall be in danger of hell fire.* The word used here is the same word the Psalmist used when he said, "The fool hath said in his heart, There is no God" (PSALM 14:1). Such a man as this was an immortal, loose-living, thoroughly disreputable person. To call a man a fool was to destroy his good name and reputation, and for this one was liable to the severest judgment of all— not the judgment of the village courts, or even the judgment of the high Sanhedrin; but this person was subject to the judgment of Almighty God. This certainly includes the tale-bearing gossip who kills a person's reputation. Jesus is saying that such an action is a hell-deserving sin. As George Meredith said, "A gossip is a beast of prey who does not even wait for the death of the victim he devours." The sin, Jesus is pointing out, is not so much in the action as in the attitude.

Be Reconciled

Then He tells us: ". . . if thou bring thy gift to the altar, and rememberest that thy brother hath ought against thee; Leave there thy gift before the altar, and go thy way; first be reconciled to thy brother, and then come and offer thy gift." As we read the Bible we know that the chief tragedy of sin is that it separates men from God—it breaks the relationship. The whole purpose of the sacrifice upon the altar was to restore that broken relationship, but if one had a broken relationship with his brother, he could not hope to bring about a restored relationship with God until first the relationship with his brother was restored. One cannot be right with God until he is right with his fellow man. Therefore, any worship of God is meaningless as long as there is an unrepaired human relationship in our hearts.

We all know that there are times when the other person will not accept reconciliation even after one has confessed, apologized, and done everything possible. That is not the point. The point is that we must rid our own hearts of the wrong feeling and do all we can to restore the relationship. Now, if the other person refuses a right relationship, at least the one who attempted the restoration is cleared and free to come back and kneel before God.

Irving R. Stone in *Love Is Eternal* has an account of a conversation between Abraham Lincoln's wife, Mary Todd, and Parker, the man who was supposed to guard the President the night he was shot: "Parker entered, a heavy-faced man with half-closed lids. He trembled.

" 'Why were you not at the door to keep the assassin out?' she asked fiercely.

"Parker hung his head. 'I have bitterly repented it. But I did not believe that any one would try to kill so good a man in such a public place. The belief made me careless. I was attracted by the play, and did not see the assassin enter the box.'

" 'You should have seen him. You had no business to be careless.' She fell back on the pillow, covered her face

· *59*

with her hands. 'Go now. It's not you I can't forgive, it's the assassin.'

" 'If Pa had lived,' said Tad, 'he would have forgiven the man who shot him. Pa forgave everybody.' "

Maybe Tad put his finger on the reason why America has so taken Abraham Lincoln to its heart. He was like Him who said, "Father, forgive them; for they know not what they do" (LUKE 23:34).

Adultery—Marriage—Divorce

Ye have heard that it was said by them of old time, Thou shalt not commit adultery:

But I say unto you, That whosoever looketh on a woman to lust after her hath committed adultery with her already in his heart.

And if thy right eye offend thee, pluck it out, and cast it from thee: for it is profitable for thee that one of thy members should perish, and not that thy whole body should be cast into hell.

And if thy right hand offend thee, cut it off, and cast it from thee: for it is profitable for thee that one of thy members should perish, and not that thy whole body should be cast into hell.

It hath been said, Whosoever shall put away his wife, let him give her a writing of divorcement:

But I say unto you, That whosoever shall put away his wife, saving for the cause of fornication, causeth her to commit adultery: and whosoever shall marry her that is divorced committeth adultery (MATTHEW 5:27-32).

Just as Jesus went beyond murder to anger, now He goes beyond adultery to lust; then He proclaims the fact that it is not the action but the attitude—the inner thought—that counts the most. The thing we must keep in mind is: sin is a matter of one's mind and heart. Our actions are merely the expressions of our inward sin. And, of course, we all realize that our Lord was not condemning the normal human desires which God put into people. What He was condemning was the deliberate intention to lust. You remember it was Martin Luther who said, "We cannot keep the birds from flying over our heads, but we can keep them from building a nest in our hair."

To emphasize the importance of our inner thoughts, our Lord uses very drastic illustrations, and talks about "plucking out" the eye that offends us or "cutting off" our right hand when it offends. Of course, the words are not to be taken literally. If I were to cut out my tongue, it would keep me from saying wrong things, but on the other hand it would destroy my ability to say kind and helpful things. If I pluck out my eye, it would keep me from seeing the dirty and the suggestive, but also it would keep me from seeing the beautiful and the true. If I cut off my hand, it would keep me from hitting someone in anger, but it would also prevent me from extending it in a firm handclasp of friendship.

In this passage, our Lord is emphasizing the fact that we must deal sternly with our inner desires and feelings, and hold them in complete check. And how is this to be done? By saying to ourselves, "We will not think about this?" The victory cannot be gained in that way. For thirty-five years, St. Anthony lived the life of a hermit, struggling with his temptations. One night the devil took upon him the shape of a woman and imitated all of her acts before him. St. Anthony never did reach the point where he could overcome that.

Let me quote a passage from the writings of Dr. Clovis Chappell, which shows a better way: "The little schoolhouse that I attended years ago was surrounded by a great grove of scrubby black oak. These trees had a wonderful way of clinging to their leaves. When the frost killed other leaves and cut them from the boughs of the trees, these oak leaves still clung, though they were as dead as any that lay on the ground. Then came the sharp winds of winter. But, even they were powerless to break the hold of these dead leaves. Still later came the snow and the sleet and the ice, but their efforts were equally futile. But one day a wonderful surgeon clipped all those leaves away. Who was that surgeon? His name was Spring. Springtime got into the heart of those oaks and the sap rose up and the new leaves pushed out and said to the old dead leaves: 'This is my place.' And thus Christ will save us. Therefore, this I say, 'Walk in the spirit and you shall not fulfil the lust of the flesh.' "

Dr. Thomas Chalmers, the great Scot preacher, used to talk about "the expulsive power of a new affection."

Now, we come to one of the statements of our Lord that has caused untold concern in the hearts of many people. It brings up the whole matter of divorce. Is divorce ever permissible? If one has been divorced, and then marries again, is he living in sin?

Jesus said, *I say unto you, That whosoever shall put away his wife, saving for the cause of fornication, causeth her to commit adultery: and whosoever shall marry her that is divorced committeth adultery.* These words were laid down in a very definite day in which definite situations existed. In that day a woman had no rights; in the sight of the law she was merely a thing. Her husband

62 ·

had absolute power over her, and with just a word he could divorce her; there was no court that would protect her. Jesus would have the people know that marriage is the most sacred of all relations in life, and something not to be taken lightly at all. However, the situation to which He addressed these words has undergone a great change.

A bright and attractive young man came into my office; he was obviously very worried. He and his wife had been very happily married for some five years. One day, he read the words of Christ in reference to the marriage of a divorced person. When his wife was twenty years old, she had married another man; they lived together for about a year, and then he deserted her. He simply told her he was through and left. He gave her no support and no help in any way. After waiting almost another year, all the time being willing to take him back and try again, and hoping he would return, the woman finally decided that her marriage was over. So she went to court and got a divorce on the grounds of desertion. Sometime after that, she and the young man who came to see me met each other, and after a time, they fell in love and were married. Their marriage had been extremely good until he read the statement and became worried over it. He wanted to know if he should immediately divorce his wife, even though he loved her dearly. He felt that, in the light of Jesus' statement, he and his wife had no right to be married.

I happen to be a minister in the Methodist Church, and so I read to him the paragraph in the *Methodist Discipline*, which is our book of law, referring to the marriage of divorced persons. The paragraph reads thus: "In view of the seriousness with which the Scriptures and the Church regard divorce, a minister may solemnize the marriage of a divorced person only when he has satisfied himself by careful counseling that: (a) the divorced person is sufficiently aware of the factors leading to the failure of the previous marriage, (b) the divorced person is sincerely preparing to make the proposed marriage truly Christian, and (c) sufficient time has elapsed for adequate preparation and counselling" (1964 edition, paragraph 356).

This did not satisfy him. He felt that no church had a right to make any statement or rule in violation of the Bible. I agreed with him fully at that point, but insisted that this was not in violation of Christ's Word. "How can that be," he said, "when the matter is stated so plainly?"

I said to him, "I cannot show you any specific reference, but I can show you something better than that, and that is the Spirit of our Christ." I turned and read to him the story of the Prodigal Son, and talked about the love of a godly father who would forgive his sinful son and restore him to the home. I turned to the eighth chapter of the Gospel According to St. John, and read to him the story of a woman who was about to be stoned to death because of the sin of adultery. Together we saw how Christ dealt with her. After her accusers were gone, gently He said to her, "Neither do I condemn thee: go, and sin no more." He was saying to her, as the father of the prodigal was saying to him, "I am willing to give you another chance."

I talked to this young man about how, over and over, Jesus spoke of the fact that He came to save sinners, that He was the "Christ of Another Chance." "Now," I asked the young husband, "do you believe that Jesus would say to your wife: 'You married when you were twenty years old, and your marriage broke up. Whether it was your fault or not is beside the point. The point is that since you've been married once, you cannot be rightfully married again. If you do ever marry again, you and the man you marry will be living in sin. I forever forbid you the opportunity of another marriage, of a home, of children. You must live the remainder of your life alone.' "

We talked about it together, and we both agreed that such would not be the attitude of the Christ we knew in the Gospels. Surely, Jesus would have said to this young man's wife: "You made a mistake, but now you are sincere in wanting another chance, and I gladly give it to you."

As one minister, I cannot see any other position than the fact that even if one has failed in a marriage, if that one is sincere, and in the right spirit enters into another marriage, that marriage will have the blessing of God. I cannot feel that if one steals or lies, or even commits murder, God will forgive him, but the same God will never forgive one who has made a mistake in his or her marriage. I used to think that the words in the ceremony, "till death us do part," referred to the death of the physical body; but, across the years, after counseling with many, many people, I've come to realize that some other things can die, too. Respect can die. Love can die. Hope can die. And a marriage can die. Realizing this fact, it behooves every married couple to give their very best in keeping their marriage alive. But, sometimes, even the best efforts of one or both have failed, and the law of our land provides a way out. I do not feel that such unhappy people are beyond God's mercy.

Having said this, though, let us re-emphasize the fact that marriage is the most important relationship in one's life, and when that relationship is broken, it leaves deep scars on the person. The saddest words the Lord ever spoke were these: "The foxes have holes, and the birds of the air have nests; but the Son of man hath not where to lay his head" (MATTHEW 8:20). One of the heaviest burdens He bore was the fact that He did not have a home. Through the years I have tried to help many couples persevere in their marriage, and many of them have succeeded. Edgar A. Guest was certainly right when he said, "It takes a heap o' livin' in a house t' make it home."

When two people marry, they should be in love; that first romantic love is a thrilling and beautiful experience. Marriage means that two people have given themselves to each other, and decided to go the same way together. In her book *Glimpses of the Moon*, Edith Wharton has one of the characters saying: "The point is that we are married . . . married. Doesn't that mean something to you, something—inexorable? It does to me. I didn't dream it would—in just that way. But all I can say is that I suppose the people who don't feel it aren't really married."

Marriage, however, is based on more than just that "inexorable" feeling. It must be a growing experience in which two people:

> . . . share each other's woes,
> Each other's burdens bare,
> And often for each other flows
> The sympathizing tear.

That first romantic love is nothing compared with the strength of the love that grows as two people walk down life's path together.

Perseverance—
Appreciation—Prayer

As a minister I have conducted many funerals, and every one, I feel, is the saddest. Sorrow never becomes routine. One never becomes accustomed to a broken heart. I've stood with children as we buried their mother, with a young couple as we buried their baby. But, to me, the most painful is to see a man and his wife—who have developed this love over a period of years—separated.

In order to develop this love, there are many things we must do. First, there is perseverance. A couple must have their money in common; marriage counselors have told me that money problems cause more breaks in marriages than any other single thing. A couple must build other things in common, too. Walter Lippmann once said, "Love and nothing else soon becomes nothing else." As couples dream and plan together, pray and work together, spend their money and rear their children together, little by little they become as one, inseparable, each finding completeness in the other. A happy marriage requires a lifetime of perseverance. It certainly is never to be entered into lightly, and never to be given up lightly.

Not only does marriage require a perseverance; in the second place, it requires appreciation of one for the other. A girl wrote to Dorothy Dix, asking the question, "How can I hold the love of my husband?" She received a very wise answer: "Learn 400 ways of saying, 'I think you are wonderful.'" When two people marry, each of them has faults and each also has virtues. During their courtship and the beginning of their marriage, they are inclined to emphasize and appreciate the virtues of each other. But as time goes by, each is inclined to see more and more of the faults of the other, and to set out to correct them. That is when the trouble usually begins. Again and again, I have said to married couples, "Stop criticizing each other, and stop trying to remake each other. You saw enough of each other to cause you to want to marry. Now, keep emphasizing and express an

· 67

appreciation for that." We are never going to make our wives or our husbands perfect. But it does help immeasurably, in holding the love of one for the other, to express appreciation.

Not only does marriage require perseverance and appreciation; in the third place, marriage requires prayer. It is often said that couples who pray together stay together. First, every couple contemplating marriage should remember these words of Christ: "What therefore God hath joined together . . ." (MATTHEW 19:6), and they should make their marriage ceremony a spiritual experience. Also, every married couple should remember these words from the Scriptures: "Except the Lord built the house, they labour in vain that build it . . ." (PSALM 127:1). Marriage is of God, and God must be in it from the beginning, and all the way, if it is to succeed.

Let no person say, after reading the comments in this section concerning divorce, that "the author believes in divorce." I do not believe in divorce, any more than I believe in death. It is the duty of man to cherish and develop the life that God has given him as long as he possibly can. Also, it is our duty before God to give our very best to our marriage.

Telling the Truth

Again, ye have heard that it hath been said by them of old time, Thou shalt not forswear thyself, but shalt perform unto the Lord thine oaths:

But I say unto you, Swear not at all; neither by heaven; for it is God's throne:

Nor by the earth; for it is his footstool: neither by Jerusalem; for it is the city of the great King.

Neither shalt thou swear by thy head, because thou canst not make one hair white or black.

But let your communication be, Yea, yea; Nay, nay: for whatsoever is more than these cometh of evil (MAT-THEW 5:33-37).

In Jesus' day, people felt that if God's name were invoked with reference to a statement, then God became a partner of the statement. They felt that this gave strength to whatever they said. But Jesus is saying such a practice is neither desirable nor necessary. In the first place, God already is a part of every person and every word he speaks, and a man should recognize that fact. Whether one actually uses God's name or not, he is under the obligation to tell the truth, and a man's character should make it unnecessary to invoke God's name.

Some have taken this to mean that they should not even take an oath in court, as a witness; that is a misinterpretation. But it does mean that when one has the true spirit of God inside his heart, then his words will always be the truth. In fact, without this inner godliness, the taking of an oath does not matter, anyway.

It has been told that, during the Korean conflict, when members of the Army Intelligence Corps often used the polygraph (lie detector) to determine whether some of the North Koreans they were questioning were telling the truth, they turned up this fact: if a man had had much contact with the Christian faith, the lie detector test would work; but if a man knew nothing of Christianity, the machine simply was of no value—to such a man, lying was so much a part of his life, that there was no sense of guilt to give him away.

Truthfulness certainly begins in the conscience of a person. When one becomes a Christian, he or she might very well say, as one of the characters said in Ellen Glasgow's book *The Deliverer:* "I hate lies, I've had so many of them, and I shall speak the truth hereafter, no matter what comes of it. Anything is better than a long, wearing falsehood, or than those hideous little shams that we are always afraid to touch for fear they would melt and show us our own nakedness. That is what I loath about my life. And that is what I've done with now forever." Christ in the heart frees one from the sham of deceit and falsehood.

Returning Good for Evil

Ye have heard that it hath been said, An eye for an eye, and a tooth for a tooth:

But I say unto you, That ye resist not evil: but whosoever shall smite thee on thy right cheek, turn to him the other also.

And if any man will sue thee at the law, and take away thy coat, let him have thy cloke also.

And whosoever shall compel thee to go a mile, go with him twain.

Give to him that asketh thee, and from him that would borrow of thee turn not thou away (MATTHEW 5:38-42).

The essence of this section of the Sermon on the Mount is: Never insist on your rights. Jesus never simply commanded, "Do your duty," but, "Do also what is not your duty." He began by citing one of the most ancient laws known to man: *An eye for an eye, and a tooth for a tooth.* That old law of tit-for-tat is as old as civilization

70 ·

itself. But when the Spirit of Christ enters into a man, his actions become different; not, how can I get even? but, how can I go beyond what is required of me? is the spirit of the Christian. The old principle of vengeance is replaced by the spirit of nonresentment and nonretaliation: *Turn to him the other cheek; let him have thy cloke also; go the second mile; do not turn away from those who come to you in need.*

The Second Mile

Jesus gives four illustrations here to emphasize this very important point in Christian living. Each of the four mean essentially the same thing, so let us lift up one of these: ... *whosoever shall compel thee to go a mile, go with him twain [two].* In that day, Palestine had been conquered by Rome. Not only did Rome exact heavy taxes, and hold the people under strict bondage; but also never let them forget that they were at all times subject to Roman orders. Palestine was occupied by Roman soldiers who constantly demanded obedience.

One of the most annoying laws was the one which allowed a soldier to compel any citizen to carry his pack for one mile. A man might be hurrying on some important mission; a soldier would see him, and demand, "Pick up this pack of mine, and carry it a mile." That was a humiliating experience. A man would not go one step farther than the law demanded. People must have thought Jesus crazy when He said that they should go still a second mile; but He was giving men something to live by. The first mile was compulsory, the second mile was voluntary: the first mile one must go, the second mile one chooses to go; the first mile was the mile of duty, the second mile was the mile of privilege. Let us note three important principles laid down here.

(1) It is the second mile which eliminates the drudgery of life. William James spoke about "our first layer of fatigue." One may push and work to the point of exhaustion, and the great psychologist said that most people operate within the limits of this first fatigue; they never really accomplish much. He said that beyond this first level there is an inexhaustible power awaiting one who taps it. Runners on a track team speak of catching their "second breath." Just as airplanes can break through the "sound barrier," so people can break through the "fatigue barrier." Many people go through life doing only those things they are compelled to do. For them life is a hard experience, and they are constantly tired. Others go beyond the call of duty and freely give themselves. They find life to be a stimulating, thrilling adventure. All of life may be divided into two parts: the first mile of compulsion, and the second mile of consecration. In the first mile, one is constantly demanding his rights; on the second mile, one is looking for opportunities. The mile of compulsion is a burden; the mile of consecration is a great joy.

(2) It is on the second mile that we make the progress of life. There is never much success to be found merely in doing our duty. We are never too successful doing those things we are compelled to do. But we find great success in doing the things we want to do.

Once, a married couple having difficulties came in to counsel with me. Each of them had made a list of demands on the other. I suggested they tear up their lists and stop thinking of what they owed each other and demanded of each other, and start thinking about how much they loved each other and wanted to do for each other. Certainly in marriage, as in all of life, it is on that second mile of love where our success is known.

(3) It is on the second mile that we find life's largest reward. My father was a minister, and he used to preach often about the second mile, but the only thing I remember about his sermons was one story he told.

A man rented a house. There were no trees around it, and his wife suggested that he set out some trees. It would have been easy for him to walk down to the woods, dig up a few small trees, and set them out in the yard, but he refused. He said it was his duty to pay the rent, and that was all. The years went by, and the man never set out any trees. Every month, for twenty-seven years, he paid the rent. Then, one day, he bought the house; now it belonged to him—but there were still no trees in the yard! My father talked about how, if the man had gone just a little bit beyond his duty, he would have ended up with nice trees to give him cool shade.

(4) It is on the second mile that we have our finest rewards in our relationships with other people. As you go along through life, somebody will do you wrong. You can count on that. When someone does you wrong, there are four attitudes you may take. First, "If he hurts me, I will hurt him more"; that is vindictive vengeance. Second, "If he hurts me, I will treat him the same"; that is retribution, the old law of an eye for an eye. Third, "If he hurts me, I will ignore him, and have nothing to do with him"; that is indifference, disdain. Fourth, "If he hurts me, I will love him, and serve him"; that is the Christian way, and that is the way that brings reward.

One day, Jesus was nailed to a cross. He had been mistreated as no other man had been. His trials had not been fair; and, even as He was hanging, He was scorned and ridiculed. He had the power to strike every one of

· 73

those people dead, or even to utterly ignore them, but He did neither. Instead, He began to pray. What was His first prayer? For the good of those who had done Him wrong! He went the second mile, and on that mile multitudes have seen Him as the Saviour. He bore His cross of duty, but He went further, and in doing so He gained His greatest reward.

Love Your Enemies

Ye have heard that it hath been said, Thou shalt love thy neighbour, and hate thine enemy.

But I say unto you, Love your enemies, bless them that curse you, do good to them that hate you, and pray for them which despitefully use you, and persecute you;

That ye may be the children of your Father which is in heaven: for he maketh his sun to rise on the evil and on the good and sendeth rain on the just and on the unjust.   For if ye love them which love you, what reward have ye? do not even the publicans the same?

And if ye salute your brethren only, what do ye more than others? do not even the publicans so? (MATTHEW 5:43-47).

To love one's neighbor and hate one's enemy is a natural thing to do, but Jesus is calling for the unnatural, and saying, "Love your enemies." The question immediately arises: Can one command love?

To answer that question, we must realize that there are two words used in the New Testament to express "love." The distinction is brought out in the Latin translation, for there are two Latin words for "love." The great Cicero used both these words in this sentence: "I do not

74   ·

esteem the man only, but I love him." Antonius used the same two words in one sentence when, at the funeral of Caesar, he declared, "Ye loved him as a father, and ye esteemed him as a benefactor." One of the words means "warm, instinctive affection." Certainly we are not commanded to love our enemies in this way. This type of love is a matter of the emotions and not of the will, and the emotions cannot be commanded. Loving your enemy does not mean "liking" him; nor does it mean blinding yourself to his faults. But we can love people whom we do not like.

What Jesus means by loving our enemies is that we are commanded to adopt a sustained and unbreakable good will toward them. It helps us in this to realize that the actions and the person are not always the same thing. Sometimes we ourselves do something of which we are ashamed, and we explain, "That was not the real I," or, "I didn't realize what I was doing," or, "I'm ashamed of what I did," or, "I was not myself." Here we clearly recognize the difference between ourselves and our actions. Now, in loving our enemies, we must do that same thing.

When we get to know a person, as distinguished from his actions, it is much easier to change our attitude. Turn again to that great novel *All Quiet on the Western Front*, and read the words as Paul Baumer is speaking: "Comrade, I do not want to kill you. If you jumped in here again, I would not do it, if you would be sensible, too. But you were only an idea to me before, an abstraction that lived in my mind and called forth its appropriate response. It was that abstraction that I stabbed. But now, for the first time, I see you are a man like me. I thought of your hand-grenades, of your bayonet, of your rifle; now, I see your life, and your face and our fellowship.

Forgive me, comrade. We always see it too late. Why do they never tell us that you are just poor devils like us? That your mothers are just as anxious as ours. That we have the same fear of death, and the same dying and the same agony—forgive me, comrade; how could you be my enemy?" Yes, when we get to know the person, it's much easier to love.

Try the Opposite

Here let me use something that I have often used with those I have been counseling. When one is facing the question, "What ought I to do?" one way that helps to decide is to ask, "What would happen if I did the opposite?" Apply that here. Instead of loving your enemy, decide that you are going to hate your enemy. Do you feel that, even for one moment, that is the better course? Was Abraham Lincoln wrong when he said, "With malice toward none; with charity for all"? Did Booker T. Washington make a mistake when he said, "I am resolved that I will permit no man to narrow and degrade my soul by making me hate him"? Surely no one of us feels that Booker T. Washington would have been a better man had he returned hate for the insults he received because of the color of his skin. If we refuse to hear Christ saying, "Love your enemies," let us beware of the fact that by hating our enemies we will harm ourselves far more than we can ever hurt those enemies.

But there is something deeper here. When Christ comes into the heart and soul of a man, then that man becomes a part of all other men. Every man then becomes his neighbor. William Saroyan said it beautifully in *The Human Comedy:* "The evil man must be forgiven every day. He must be loved, because something of each of us is in the most evil man in the world. Something of him is in each of us. He is ours and we are his. None of us is separate from the other. The peasant's prayer is my prayer. The assassin's crime is my crime."

I recall an experience of mine that illustrates the fact that when Christ comes into the human heart, we can love. I was preaching in a series of revival services. One morning, a lady phoned, asking to see me. She seemed in distress, but I could not possibly free any time for her until after the service that night. I promised to talk with her then. When I did meet her, she was smiling, and so happy that she seemed to bubble over.

I asked, "Are you sure you're the lady who phoned me this morning?"

She said, "Yes, but I don't need your help now, so I won't keep you."

I said, "Lady, when a person has changed as completely as you have, I want to know what happened." So, we sat down in the front pew of the church, and she told me her story.

Her husband had died suddenly, leaving no money nor insurance for the support of his wife and their four children. He did have, however, a small electrical-supply business. In the business was a man the husband had trained for six years, and the woman felt she could carry on the business with that man's help. She had one competitor in that community, and he tried to buy her out, offering only a fraction of what her business was worth. When she wouldn't sell, he became angry, and told her he would force her out of business. He cut prices, and did everything he could against her, yet she held on. Then, one day, the man her husband had trained told her he was quitting. He was going to work for the competitor, who had offered him more money than the woman could pay.

She carried on by herself as best she could, but it was a struggle. Sometimes her children did not have enough to eat. Worse was the hatred she had in her heart against the man who had hurt her. Hate is poison for both our souls and our bodies, and she knew that; yet she could not seem to do anything about it. It was in that situation she had phoned me that morning. That night she arranged for a neighbor to sit with her children, and she came to church to talk with me about it after the service.

My sermon that night was on the cross. I talked about how, through the power of mental television (imagination and memory), we can actually see back across the years. In detail I described His praying in Gethsemane, the coming of the soldiers, the betraying kiss of one He had trusted, and His trials before Herod and Pilate. I told about His humiliation before that mob as they stripped off His clothes, how they drove in the nails, hung Him up to die, and then spat on Him, mocked and ridiculed Him.

I took about forty-five minutes to describe that picture as vividly as I could. Then I said, "Listen! He is about to speak!" We strained our ears and across the centuries His voice came clear and strong, saying, "Father, forgive them." Then I invited those present to come to the altar and pray.

The woman told me that, as she knelt, the only thing she could think of was the man she hated so. She found herself praying for him. She prayed the prayer the Master prayed, and she felt cleansed and whole again. She told me how she had no fear of the future. When Christ comes into our hearts, we can love even as He loved.

Bless Your Critics

Our Lord said, . . . *bless them that curse you.* . . .
Oftentimes, we completely exaggerate the harm someone
may do to us. For a number of years, I have written for
daily newspapers, and a column in the paper will draw a
considerable amount of mail, not always complimentary.
It used to upset me when the newspaper printed an unfavorable "letter to the editor" about my column, but now
I have learned that those unfavorable comments are often
the ones that get me the best publicity and support.

When Longfellow published *Hiawatha*, it was greeted
with both praise and scorn. Especially did a newspaper in
Boston condemn this literary work in such vile tones that
one day the publisher said to Longfellow, "These atro-
cious libels must be stopped!"

Longfellow calmly asked, "By the way, how is *Hiawatha* selling?"

"Wonderfully," replied the publisher, "no other poem
of yours has had such a sale."

"Then," answered Longfellow, "suppose we let these
people go on advertising it."

The Critics of Jesus

Let us recall that it was from the critics of Jesus that
He received some of His greatest compliments. Often
you can judge a man better by what his enemies say
about him than by what his friends say; so let me call the
enemies of Christ to the witness stand and hear their
testimony.

Number one: "Never man spake like this man" (JOHN 7:46). These were the words of the officers who were sent to arrest Him. He gave to the world a new language, a language of hope which pointed to a better way.

The religious language of that day was full of prohibitions. There were countless laws, and over and over the people were told that they would be cursed and punished for breaking those laws. St. Mark tells us: "Jesus came into Galilee, preaching the gospel [good news] of the kingdom of God" (1:14). Eighty-eight times He told people how they could be "blessed." His words were not to condemn, but to help, and He put them so simply and winsomely that even "the common people heard him gladly" (MARK 12:37).

Number two: ". . . behold, the world is gone after him" (JOHN 12:19). This was the testimony of jealous Pharisees. They were saying that when people came to know Him, they followed Him. The authorities killed Him, but the world is still going after Him. Wesley sang,

> O, for a thousand tongues to sing,
> My great redeemer's praise.

Today His praise is being sung in more than a thousand tongues; in fact, in two hundred more than a thousand tongues: His words are now translated into 1,200 languages and dialects.

Number three: "Is not this the carpenter . . . ?" (MARK 6:3). These words were said sneeringly by people of His home town. They were right. The carpenter can take rough-hewn timbers and make of them a castle. Jesus is taking men and women who are sinners, redeeming and refining them, and using them to build "colonies of heaven." He is fashioning men and women into likenesses of Himself, and with them He is building the Kingdom of God on earth.

Number four: "He saved others; himself he cannot save" (MATTHEW 27:42). This was said by those who were seeking to mock Him, but they were only mocking themselves. To become a Saviour of the suffering, He had to become a suffering Saviour. Poor, blind, selfish men! They are the ones who were not saved. They refused to listen when He told them: "He that findeth his life shall lose it: and he that loseth his life for my sake shall find it" (MATTHEW 10:39). We can never save ourselves except by giving ourselves to something greater than ourselves. In the saving of others, we do save ourselves.

Number five: "Then said the Jews, Behold how he loved him!" (JOHN 11:36). This was spoken by His critics as they watched Him weeping at the grave of Lazarus. And not only Lazarus did He love; He loved the young ruler, the sinful woman, the poor beggar at the gate. Not only did He love John, who loved Him; also He loved Judas, who betrayed Him. Not only did He love the little children, who rushed into His arms; also He loved those who nailed Him to the cross. And, best of all, He loves me. So we sing, "O, Love, that wilt not let me go."

Number six: "This is Jesus the king of the Jews" (MATTHEW 27:37). They nailed those words above His head, but almost two thousand years later multitudes of people stand and sing, "King of kings, forever and ever." No other king has commanded even a fraction of the following He commands today. He is *The King*.

Number seven: ". . . he made himself the Son of God" (JOHN 19:7). This was a charge hurled against Him at His trial. Today, millions are still saying it. Someone has said: "All the armies that ever marched, all the navies that were ever built, all the parliaments that have ever sat, and all the kings that have ever ruled, put together, have not affected the life of man upon this earth like this one solitary personality." What is the explanation? Napoleon said, "I know men, and I know Jesus Christ was no man." He was truly God.

Do — More

"And if ye salute your brethren only, what do ye more than others? do not even the publicans so?" (MATTHEW 5:47).

In that day, the usual salute, or greeting, among friends was the word *Shalom*, which means "Peace and prosperity be unto you." This was more than a mere greeting; it was a prayer which was usually reserved for one's friends. But the Christian prays not only for those he loves, but for every one he meets, and when one has the spirit of Christ within him, he is always the first to give the salute. It is easy to pray for those we love, but it is right to pray for every person we meet.

". . . what do ye more than others?" When Jesus spoke those words, I suspect that He put the emphasis on the word "do," because the Christian faith always leads to positive action. Oftentimes, we deal with the "don'ts" of life, and to my mind, that is a slander against the Christian faith. Christianity is an exciting way of living; it is a firm conviction that evil can be overcome with good. In the early days of the faith, it was not the preaching that won the people, but rather the way those Christians lived and ministered to those about them. If one were to make a list of all the things that have been done in the name of Christ, that list would fill many, many volumes.

Or, as Jesus spoke that sentence, He might have emphasized the word "more." So many people approach life with the thought of seeing how little they can do, rather than how much. Walter Russell Bowie, in his book *Great Men of the Bible*, writes: "The hack worker goes dully along the narrow groove of his immediate responsibility, giving no more than he is paid for, taking no interest in anything beyond what he is obliged to do and never turning an intelligent and inquiring thought toward what might be a better relationship of the thing he is doing to the larger works of which that thing is a part. But the man who is marked out for mastery has a ranging mind. He sees the next thing beyond that which he knows already, which it would be worthwhile to learn and he is not too lazy to make the extra effort to learn it." Study the successful people in life, and you will find that they never lived on the minimum plan.

The Christian is kinder in his thoughts and actions than others are. The Christian stands up to the adversities of life better than others do. The Christian sacrifices more for the great ideals than others do. The Christian puts more into life than is required.

The Perfect Life

Be ye therefore perfect, even as your Father which is in heaven is perfect (MATTHEW 5:48).

For many people, this is one of the most puzzling statements Jesus ever made. Conscious of our own imperfections and of our past sins, how can we expect to be perfect? There is a tendency on the part of many to say, "Well, I have already failed here, and there is no need for me to consider this idea further." But note, the verb here is future: *Be ye therefore perfect.* . . . It is not looking to the past or even to the present, but to the future; and here we have the very essence of religion. The natural sciences seek to know the true world *about* man. Anthropology and sociology seek to know the true world *of* man. Politics and government seek to know the true world *for* man. Psychology seeks to know the true world *in* man. Philosophy summarizes the truth of the *life* of man. Religion is not only concerned with the past and the present of man, but is also concerned with the world yet *before* and *beyond* man.

This passage is saying to us, "Hold fast to your ideals." One of the dangers we face is the surrendering of our ideals. In Aldous Huxley's book *Point-Counterpoint*, one of the characters says, "You can't cart a wagon-load of ideals and romanticism about with you these days. When you travel by airplane, you must leave your heavy baggage behind. The good old-fashioned soul was all right when people lived slowly. But it's too ponderous nowadays. There's no room for it in an airplane." There is one of our present-day dangers: life is too hurried, and we decide we do not have time for dreams and ideals.

But this same Aldous Huxley, in another one of his books, *Antic Hay*, has another of his characters condemning this idea: "You're afraid of ideals. That's what it is. You daren't admit to having dreams . . . ideals—they are not sufficiently genteel for you civilized young men. You've outgrown that sort of thing. No dream, no religion, no morality."

There is a tendency for us to say, "Why should imperfect individuals concern themselves about impossible ideals?" And we just mark this verse out of our Bibles with the statement: "It just can't be done." At the beginning of the New Year, we make resolutions, only to see them broken. There is a tendency, as the years go by, to give up the idea of the resolutions altogether. We have set goals for ourselves, only to fall far short in discouragement.

We look at the world about us and see how many of the ideals have failed. For example, we have dreamed of a world of peace, and yet, even now, we see our boys going off to war. We think of so many conditions in our society against which men have fought through the centuries, and yet the evil is still there. We have been disappointed in some we trusted. The margin between the declarations and the demonstrations of both ourselves and our fellow men has become so wide that we feel, "What's the use of these impossible ideals any longer?"

But the true Christian never gives up. In *A Lantern in Her Hand*, Bess Streeter Aldrich tells of Abby Deal, who dreamed about her new home on the Nebraska prairies. She desired a picket fence around the yard—a nice fence, painted white, with red hollyhocks and blue larkspur alongside it. "You're quite a dreamer, Abby-girl," said her husband, Will.

Abby replied, "You have to dream, Will . . . you have to dream things out. It keeps a kind of ideal before you. You see it first in your mind, and then you set about to try to make it like the ideal. If you want a garden—why, I guess you've got to dream a garden."

Whenever I see a baby, I think: "Here is a perfect human being. This little one has never said or thought or done anything that is wrong. It is absolutely perfect." But suppose that baby remained as it is? As time went on, that would be a great tragedy. The glory of a little baby is that it has a lifetime before it in which to grow and develop. There is almost no greater tragedy on this earth than a retarded child, one who never attains true growth and maturity. So, in the Christian life, we are never concerned altogether with what we are; our greater concern is what we may become, and that is what our dreams are all about.

In one of his speeches, the late President John F. Kennedy repeated a question that had been asked of him: "Why do we try to go to the moon?" His answer was: "Because it is there." And the Christian is ever an unsatisfied person, always reaching for things well above him.

I do not feel that Jesus really expected us to obtain perfection in this life. It is as Browning said:

> . . . a man's reach should exceed his grasp,
> Or what's a heaven for?

As I see it, the true interpretation of our Lord's words, *Be ye therefore perfect*, does not apply altogether to our actions and our lives, but rather to the desires of our heart. We may never attain perfection, but there is such a thing as attaining a perfect desire to be perfect. One of the differences between a swine and sheep is this: the hog falls in the mudhole, and wallows in it, and enjoys it; the sheep falls in the mudhole, but is not happy there, and struggles to get out. The Christian is constantly struggling to rise above the mud, the wrongs, the imperfections of this life.

In my own church, when one is ordained a minister, among other questions this one is asked: "Are you going on to perfection?" The answer is: "I am earnestly striving after it." Through the years I have come to know many ministers, and I have yet to find one who ever attained perfection. I am sorry to say that I have known some who quit striving for it. There is the great tragedy. None of us Christians will ever become perfect, but we can always keep trying, and that is what God expects.

IV

VI

IV

The Motives
of the Christian

IN DEALING WITH the motives that are to control
our actions, our Lord specifically referred to three areas
of Christian activity: giving, praying, and fasting. These
were the three great religious works of the Jew, and
were the foundations upon which the good life was
based.

Giving

*Take heed that ye do not your alms before men, to be
seen of them: otherwise ye have no reward of your Father which is in heaven.*

*Therefore when thou doest thine alms, do not sound a
trumpet before thee, as the hypocrites do in the synagogues and in the streets, that they may have glory of
men. Verily I say unto you, They have their reward.*

*But when thou doest alms, let not thy left hand know
what thy right hand doeth:*

*That thine alms may be in secret: and thy Father
which seeth in secret himself shall reward thee openly*
(MATTHEW 6:1-4).

Take heed—be careful what your motive is, because the wrong motive can ruin even the finest service or the most beautiful gift. For an illustration of this fact, look at a scene in Jesus' own life. Death was closing in upon Him; the crowds which had applauded Him were about to cry, "Crucify Him!"; His own disciples had gone to sleep; He had asked God to "let this cup pass" (MATTHEW 26:39); but His own Father did not see fit to save Him from death. Across the hill came the soldiers to take Him. Then one of His disciples stepped forward. It was Judas. St. Mark records: ". . . he goeth straightway to him, and saith, Master, master; and kissed him" (MARK 14:45). That might have been the moment that a man rose to the highest height to which any man has ever risen on this earth. Or it might have been the moment when a man sank to the lowest depth in all the history of human living. Which was it? You cannot decide by merely looking at the act. You must decide by discovering the motives. Why did Judas kiss Jesus? Did Judas stand forth in that moment to own his Master and express his love? Or was he disowning and betraying his Master? It isn't the act. It is the motive that determines.

> The last temptation is the greatest treason:
> To do the right deed for the wrong reason
>
> *Murder in the Cathedral*, T. S. Eliot

What are our motives for giving? Giving is a blessed thing, but oftentimes we receive no reward for our giving because we do it for the wrong reason.

(1) Sometimes we give because we are in a situation where we are forced. In nearly every city there is a

United Fund or a Community Chest. One of the major ways of raising money for this great community service is through the payroll deduction plan of large companies. The bosses simply go to all the people and say, "How much do you want to give this year?" A worker might not want to give anything, but he feels that he would be disliked in his company if he did not give, and so he names an amount to be withheld each payday from his salary.

People often find themselves in a somewhat similar position in the church. At the beginning of the church year, each home is visited and the members are asked, "How much do you intend to give to the church this year?" Many people put down some amount, not because they really want to give, but because they just cannot avoid it.

(2) Sometimes people give, as Jesus pointed out, "to be seen." Such giving is done to enhance their own prestige and position. Most of us have been in meetings where a public collection was taken up. The one taking the collection would ask, "Who will give a hundred dollars? Raise your hand!" Some would raise their hands. The collection would proceed as the speaker went on asking for various amounts. I personally have always felt that such a offering was an unchristian way of raising money. Yet, there have been times when that was the most successful way. There are always some people who will not give unless everybody is going to know that they have given.

The Lord said, . . . *do not sound a trumpet* . . . when you give. He did not mean that literally, but meant what we mean when we say, "Do not blow your own horn."

(3) Another appeal which is used often is that the cause needs or deserves the contribution. It is a common

practice in our churches to print the budget of the church and pass it our among the members with the appeal: "Here is what your church needs. Therefore, you ought to give." Or, in seeking money for some charity cause, we point out the great needs and the pitiful circumstances, and say, "This ought to cause us to give." Neither is this the proper motive.

(4) There is really only one motive for giving. St. Paul clearly states it in these words: "And though I bestow all my goods to feed the poor, and though I give my body to be burned, and have not charity [love], it profiteth me nothing" (1 CORINTHIANS 13:3). The only true motive for giving is that it becomes the overflowing of love in our own hearts. We give not because we are forced to, or to enhance our position, or even because of some great need. We give because of the love within our hearts, and love always expresses itself.

Some of the happiest memories of my own life are when, as a child, I went with my father around to his churches. My father was a country preacher who served rural churches during most of his ministry. I can remember when he drove a horse and buggy, and I would ride with him. Never will I forget one Sunday morning when we were driving in the buggy to one of his churches. Along the way there lived an old, retired schoolteacher whom everybody called "Professor Miller." He was sitting out by the side of the road in front of his house, waiting for my father to come along. My father stopped, and they talked for a few moments. Then Professor Miller took out of his pocket two fifty-cent pieces and handed them to my father. He said, "I want to make a contribution to the church for my wife and for myself."

My father knew of the circumstances of this dear old man. He knew that he and his wife barely had enough to exist on, and so he said to him. "Professor Miller, I appreciate this gift, but we are coming out real good in the church this year, and we do not really need it, so I want you to keep the money."

Of course, my father meant well, but the old teacher looked up at him and said, "Brother Allen, would you deny me the privilege of giving to my Lord?" He was not giving because he thought the church needed it, nor because anybody expected him to, nor to gain any glory. He was giving because it was in his heart, and he felt compelled to express it.

The Rewards of Giving

Giving with the right motive does bring rewards. There are those who want to leave the reward motive completely out of the Christian life, but Jesus does not do it. Three times, in the sixth chapter of Matthew, He refers to rewards which God gives. We do not do things to get the reward, but the reward comes when we do the right things in the right way. We have heard some say, "God will not let us outgive Him." And they go ahead to point out that, if we give, God will give it back to us. I do not believe that is always true—and certainly, I know we should never give with that motive in mind. The Psalmist says, "I have been young, and now am old; yet have I not seen the righteous forsaken, nor his seed begging bread" (PSALM 37:25). Come to think about it, neither have I ever seen the righteous begging. I do believe there is a providence overshadowing those who are faithful to God, but that is not the motive for giving. But there are some higher and greater rewards.

First, through giving, we gain a sense of living. What

are the highest joys that parents receive? Is it not in sacrificing for their children? At times, some parents may feel that they are burdened by the things their child requires, and the things they have to give it and do for it. But suppose that child developed an illness and died? As the parents watched the last breath go out of that child, and realized they could do nothing more for it, actually a part of the life of the mother and the father would die, too. The opportunity to give is really the opportunity to live.

Whenever an opportunity to give is presented to you, be thankful, because that opportunity is opening channels of life to you. The parish priest in A. S. M. Hutchinson's *The Uncertain Trumpet* said it beautifully: "You do not love the life down here because, as you say, you are living for it . . . because when you are here, you are giving; and because life, real life, living, is giving. When you are taking, only taking, you are not living, you are slowly dying."

The second reward of giving is that it strengthens our own lives. One never gives without receiving something more valuable in return. One of the most often quoted verses in the Bible, in reference to giving, in this one: "Bring ye all the tithes into the storehouse, that there may be meat in mine house, and prove me now herewith, saith the Lord of hosts, if I will not open you the windows of heaven, and pour you out a blessing, that there shall not be room enough to receive it" (MALACHI 3:10). Now, the blessing the Lord promises to pour out upon the giver is not necessarily a material blessing, but the promise is always that the giver will be blessed by it. Conversely, to face a situation in which one ought to give, and to turn away from it, brings hurt upon that person. This is true of every duty of life, and certainly giving is one of life's duties. When I face up to my duty and respond to it at my best, I am going to be strengthened by it. When I turn away from a duty, then I am going to be weakened by the very act of turning away.

We must not assume that we should give because it is our duty. As I have indicated, there are higher motives for giving. But, at the same time, we must also recognize that the demands of living carry with them the demands of giving.

We give because we love. But, on the other hand, sometimes giving is the pathway to love. We are familiar with the three rules of giving that have been quoted many, many times: (1) give, (2) give until it hurts, (3) give until it feels good.

In the third place, one of the great rewards of giving is that it broadens and lengthens our own lives. By giving, I am enabled to serve in many places and in many institutions in which I could not expect to be physically present. In his book *In Quest of a Kingdom*, Leslie D. Weatherhead tells a wonderful story: "The chairman of a missionary meeting claimed he was the founder of a flourishing Christian community in India, although he had never been out of England. To the amazed listeners, he said that when he was five years old, he wanted to give a penny to the missionaries, but strongly objected to putting it in a brown box. He had no proof that it ever went abroad. The local minister was a friend of the family and also a friend of an Indian missionary. So the minister, to please the child, sold him a copy of the New Testament for his penny and directed the boy how to post it to the missionary in India, having first written on the flyleaf an inscription giving the name of the boy. The missionary gave it to a poor native who had walked miles through the jungle to procure a testament, but who couldn't afford to buy one. Nothing was heard of the incident for twenty years. Then, another missionary, preaching in a jungle village to people who he thought had never previously heard the gospel message, noticed that his words were causing excited delight. Pausing in his preaching to ask questions, the preacher found that the people knew a great deal about Christ and that many were serving Him. No preacher had ever been to the village before. The little Christian community had been born through the love and life of the native who had been given the Testament—the Testament which was sold for a penny to a child of five."

Giving with the right motive does bring great and lasting rewards.

Prayer

And when thou prayest, thou shalt not be as the hypocrites are: for they love to pray standing in the synagogues and in the corners of the streets, that they may be seen of men. Verily I say unto you, They have their reward.

But thou, when thou prayest, enter into thy closet, and when thou hast shut thy door, pray to thy Father which is in secret; and thy Father which seeth in secret shall reward thee openly.

But when ye pray, use not vain repetitions, as the heathen do: for they think that they shall be heard for their much speaking.

Be not ye therefore like unto them: for your Father knoweth what things ye have need of, before ye ask him (MATTHEW 6:5-8).

Even prayer can become a meaningless and worthless experience when done with the wrong motives. In Jesus' day, prayer was one of the common experiences of life. Walk into any church at any time, and you could see numbers of people standing there, lifting their voices in prayer. Even as one walked down the street, one could see, at every corner, people engaged in prayer. The trouble was that many of those people were hypocrites. The word *hypocrite* literally means "an actor." Those people were not really praying—they were just acting. Why did they pray on the corners of the streets? Simple because there they could be seen from four directions, and actors are always seeking an audience. Likewise, many people entered the synagogue, and there, too, was a constant stream of viewers before whom they could pray. Their motive was "to be seen of men."

It is not wrong to pray publicly, and in the Sermon on the Mount our Lord warns against "hiding our light under a bushel." He urges, "Let your light so shine before men that they may see your good works." I like the story of the man who was totally deaf, yet went to church every Sunday. Someone said to him one day, "You cannot hear one word the preacher says. Why do you go to church?" His reply was. "I go to church to let people know whose side I'm on."

But the hypocrites to whom Jesus was referring had no motive other than to glorify themselves with their prayer. They really had no interest in God at all. Jesus told about a Pharisee and a publican who once went to the temple to pray. He said, "The Pharisee stood and prayed thus with himself" (LUKE 18:11). Goodspeed translates that verse to read: "The Pharisee stood up and uttered this prayer to himself. . . ." He was not praying to God at all, but to himself. He had a good eye on

· *99*

himself, a bad eye on others, and no eye on God. His prayer was just an effort to inflate his own ego; and in the same way, we pray to other people to raise our standing in their eyes.

Someone once described the prayer of a certain preacher in a Boston church thus: "It was the most eloquent prayer ever offered to a Boston audience." One can be much more concerned with the impression he makes on other people than with communion with God.

Verily I say unto you, They have their reward. It is certainly true that one can inflate his ego through prayer, and one can raise his standing in the eyes of his fellow man through the practice of holy things. But when one prays with that motive, that is the only good that comes of it—the only reward he receives. We can build churches for the glory of God—or we can build them to impress the community.

"To do the right deed for the wrong reason" is always a bad practice, and so our Lord says, . . . *enter into thy closet . . . ;* that is, find a place of prayer in which you are not seen except by God. This does not mean to go literally into a closet, or even into a room and close the door, though sometimes this is a wonderful practice. But the experience of prayer can be had even as one walks along the street, or as he sits in the midst of a large crowd. One can shut the world out even while he is in the midst of the world. The main point of prayer is to experience God.

Think of your mind as being a house with several rooms. One room of your house is your office, which represents your daily work. One may spend all of his time in that room, and never get away from the worries and problems of making a living. Another room in the house is the kitchen, in which your meals are prepared.

One may live his life on the animal level, thinking only of the satisfaction of his physical desires. Underneath the house is the cellar, which might indicate the dingy, dark areas, the secret desires for wrong, lust, and all of the other destructive emotions of men. One can live on that level. Above is the attic, which stores an accumulation of your past. One can live with old griefs and fears, old worries and regrets. In some houses, however, above the attic there is a room to which one can climb, high above the ground, which looks out toward the heavens. No matter where one's body may happen to be—walking along the street, working at the job, standing in the midst of a crowd—one can climb into this mental room high above and there commune with Him who is the Highest.

Further, our Lord warns against "repetition" and "much speaking." There was a tendency in that day just to say the same thing over and over and over, as if the length of the prayers was the thing that determined the power of the prayer. There is a wonderful conversation along this line in the book *How Green Was My Valley*, by Richard Llewellyn: " 'Keep up your spirit, Hub, for that is the heritage of a thousand generations of the great ones of the East. As your father cleans his lamp to have a good light, so clean your spirit.'

" 'And how shall it be kept clean, Mr. Gruffydd?' I asked him.

" 'By prayer, my son,' he said, 'not mumbling, or shouting, or wallowing like a hog in religious sentiments. Prayer is only another name for good, clean, direct thinking. When you pray, think well what you are saying, and make your thoughts into things that are solid. In that manner, your prayer will have strength, and that strength shall become part of you, mind, body, and spirit.' "

If someone came to me and asked, "Can you tell me the way?" I would answer, "The way where?" Likewise, in prayer, it often happens that one just rambles around in his praying, with no definite purpose or object. I have suggested to many people that in preparation for prayer they should write down exactly why they are praying and the answers they are seeking. One may write for several pages, but after he has written his thoughts, he should reduce what he has written to about fifty words. Sometime ago, I wrote a letter, which was a full page long, to a person. After I finished the letter I realized it would not reach the person in time, so instead I sent a telegram. I reduced the thought of that page-long letter into a fifteen-word telegram, and, really, I think I said it more clearly in the fifteen words than in the entire page! So, reduce your thinking to about fifty words; then, read over again and again those fifty words until they are clear in your mind. It is amazing how much clearer and easier praying becomes when we eliminate from our prayers our "repetitions" and our "much speaking." Let us remember that Jesus gave us the Lord's Prayer, which has become a model for all Christian prayer, and it contains only sixty-six words. Certainly the Lord's Prayer is an example of what He is saying.

. . . your Father knoweth what things ye have need of, before ye ask him. This being true, and we know it is true, then why go through the process of askng? Why not simply say, "Lord, You know what I need, so there is no need for me to tell You." But there is a need to tell God what we want, and to ask Him. Parents give to their children many gifts for which they do not ask: a bed in which to sleep, food to eat, clothes to wear, protection as far as possible, and many other things. On the other hand, there are some things parents cannot give to their

children unless and until they ask for them. An education is an example. Parents can give to their children an opportunity for an education, but the children must want the education before it can be given to them. I would be happy to give one of my children musical training. I could find a music teacher and pay the cost, but my child would never learn to play until that child wanted to learn to play. There are some gifts that cannot be given until someone is willing to receive them.

Likewise, God gives us many gifts for which we do not ask: the air we breathe, the sun that shines, the rain that falls. But there are many other gifts that God knows we need. Yet He cannot give them to us until we recognize our need for those gifts and are willing to receive them. The asking is the expressing of our desires, and thus, the asking is of utmost importance. All of us have missed out on many, many blessings which God has had for us, simply because we never have asked Him.

Prayers Are Answered

When one prays sincerely, he may be sure that he is always rewarded. Jesus declared, . . . *thy Father which seeth in secret shall reward thee openly.* For a number of years now, my thesis has been that there is no such thing as an unanswered prayer. Sometimes our prayers are not answered in exactly the form that we want or expect. But they always are answered.

Turn again to the twelfth chapter of II Corinthians, and read the wonderful experience of St. Paul in reference to prayer. He speaks about his "thorn in the flesh" (v. 7). We are not told what that thorn was. It might have been some physical infirmity; it might have been the fact that he was never married, and never had a home, and spent many lonely hours; it might have been a disappointment in some dear friend; it might have been the shattering of some of his hopes and dreams; it might have been one of many things. Three times Paul prayed that the thorn might be removed. I do not take it literally that he prayed merely three times. My thought is that he prayed many times. However, the thorn was not removed. Whatever it was, he bore the pain of it until his death. His prayer surely was answered but in another way: "My grace is sufficient for thee . . ." (v. 9). God did not remove the thorn, but He gave Paul the grace (strength) to bear it.

We remember the scene in Lloyd C. Douglas' novel *The Big Fisherman* where a Roman officer prayed for Peter's life. Peter was condemned to die. " 'I have prayed for you, Peter,' murmured Mencius, 'but, it hasn't done you any good.'

" 'I'm sure it has!' said Peter. 'I haven't been afraid.' "

Would you say that Mencius' prayer was not answered?

When one thinks of prayer, the name of St. Francis of Assisi quickly comes to mind. It is said that he was so close to Christ that he even bore on his body the marks of the cross. Certainly he was as close in spirit to Christ as any of the disciples who followed Him in the days of His flesh. St. Francis knew so much about prayer that he prayed one of the greatest prayers that has ever been recorded on this earth:

"Lord, make me an instrument of your peace; where there is hatred, let me sow love; where there is injury, pardon; where there is doubt, faith; where there is despair, hope; where there is darkness, light; and where there is sadness, joy.

"O Divine Master, grant that I may not so much seek to be consoled, as to console; to be understood, as to understand; to be loved, as to love; for it is in giving that we receive; it is in pardoning that we are pardoned; and it is in dying, we are born to eternal life. Amen."

What a magnificent prayer St. Francis prayed! Few people who have ever lived on this earth could really pray as he did. But, come down to the last days of his life, and the record notes that he prayed just as fervently for health to carry on his work a little while longer. Instead of health, he painfully coughed out his life with tuberculosis. Yet, who could say that St. Francis' prayer was not answered? Surely St. Francis received his reward; so did St. Paul—and so will you receive your reward when you pray.

The Lord's Prayer

After this manner therefore pray ye: Our Father which art in heaven, Hallowed be thy name.

Thy kingdom come. Thy will be done in earth, as it is in heaven.

Give us this day our daily bread.

And forgive us our debts, as we forgive our debtors.

And lead us not into temptation, but deliver us from evil: For thine is the kingdom, and the power, and the glory, for ever. Amen (MATTHEW 6:9-13).

The Lord's Prayer is recorded twice in the gospels. In Saint Luke's account (LUKE 11:1-4), we have the disciples saying to Jesus, "Lord, teach us to pray. . . ." It is important to note that this is the only thing the disciples ever asked the Lord to teach them. They never asked

Him to teach them how to perform miracles, how to organize churches, or even how to win the world. After they had seen Jesus praying, they realized that once they learned how to pray, all of these other things would come.

We know that the Sermon on the Mount is really the "set of instructions" for the disciples, and as we read this sermon we find no section teaching the disciples any other of the activities in which they would be engaged, except that of praying. Instead of giving them a lengthy discourse on the techniques of prayer, the Lord simply gave them a prayer. Really, the Lord's Prayer is a pattern to follow, and as one prays within that framework he will find himself taking hold of the power of God.

On one occasion a very disturbed and earnest man came to counsel with me. He said, "For the first time in my life, I feel the need of prayer. Now I realize I do not know how to pray. Will you teach me?"

I said to him, "Get somewhere where it is quiet and you will not be disturbed; then take the Lord's Prayer and begin to read those words. Read very slowly, thinking about what each word is saying, and letting each word stimulate your thinking. Then express in your own words the thoughts that come to you as you think the words of the Lord's Prayer." This is something I do frequently, and I find that my thoughts are stimulated in many ways by the Lord's Prayer. I really think the Lord's Prayer should be the basis of prolonged meditation on the part of all Christian people.

Our Father which art in heaven—the first step in prayer is not asking for something, but silencing the mind: "Be still, and know that I am God" (PSALM 46:10). My own father was buried in Westview Cemetery in Atlanta, Georgia. Afterwards, I was a minister in that city for twelve years, and during those years I went to that cemetery many times for funeral services. Almost without exception, after we had concluded the service, I would drive by the grave of my father, get out of my car, and just stand there for a little while. I would think about him, and many memories would crowd my mind. I would think of his character, of his goodness, of his kindness, of his love for me. That experience always left me inspired and lifted up.

So, when I begin to pray, I just like to stop and think about my heavenly Father. I think of His goodness, and His purposes, and His love for me. The beginning of prayer is centering our minds on God.

. . . *which art in heaven* . . .—that does not mean that God is sitting down in some far-off place of golden streets and gates of pearl. What Jesus had in mind was the whole creation, the entire universe. In fact, I think the better translation would be: "Who art in the universe." God is everywhere in His universe, creating, upholding it, and carrying it forward. God is where we are, and we are a part of His creative purpose. We are being undergirded by His wisdom and His love. However, as I pray these words, I like to think of John's vision of heaven as recorded in chapter 21 of the Book of Revelation. He depicts heaven as a place where "God shall wipe away all tears from their eyes; and there shall be no more death, neither sorrow, nor crying, neither shall there be any more pain . . ." (v. 4). That is such a beautiful and peaceful scene. One cannot imagine a cyclone in heaven, or an earthquake, or an automobile wreck, or a war, or any of the things that bring sorrow and pain to human life. As I think of God in this way, I feel calm in my own soul.

Hallowed be thy name—thinking of God, I feel that

· *107*

He is exalted above all things on the earth. At this part of
the prayer, one is moved to think of the words of the
great hymn:

> Holy, holy, holy! Lord, God Almighty!
> Early in the morning, our song shall rise to Thee!

We feel that the name of God is almost too sacred to
be spoken by human lips. As we feel His presence, our
hearts are filled with awe, and our ego is melted into deep
reverence. At this point, our faith becomes greatly
strengthened.

One of the Ten Commandments forbids the taking of
the name of the Lord in vain. We generally think of that
in reference to profanity, but actually the most profane
word a Christian can utter is "hopeless." The Psalmist
repeats one question twice in the same Psalm; it is this:
"Why art thou cast down, O my soul? and why art thou
disquieted in me?" Then, the Psalmist says, ". . . hope
thou in God" (PSALM 42:5). The point is, when one
believes in God, and has God in his life, he has strength
and faith. The more reverent our attitude toward God,
the stronger we are inside.

Thy kingdom come—since we began our prayer with
God, we continue to think of God as we pray. Thus, our
prayer is not "my" kingdom come, but "Thy" kingdom.
So many times, the reason one prays is that he wants
something from God, or wants God to do something,
and his prayers literally are selfish. But, when one's mind
is filled with God, he begins to think in terms of what
God wants. He begins to pray for a society in which
God would feel at home. He thinks of all the things in
our society that hurt, and he suddenly wants all those
things eliminated from our world.

Have you ever been in a group when someone said, "Let us repeat together the Lord's Prayer"? That is the tragedy—we sometimes simply "repeat" instead of pray. It does not take much effort to pray, "Thy kingdom come," but praying those words can shake us to our very foundations.

Thy will be done . . .—here again, we forget our own desires, and we put our minds upon what His desire is. All too often, what this prayer means to many people is a negative acceptance of pain, defeat, and suffering. We associate these words with our Lord's praying in Gethsemane: "Thy will be done." And then we think about His going from Gethsemane to Calvary's cross. For many of us, "God's will" and "the cross" have become synonymous terms. But, just as you will for your children life and joy and success, so God wills for His children.

. . . in earth, as it is in heaven—as we picture heaven, we picture a life completely in harmony with God. We cannot think of disobedience in heaven.

Give us this day our daily bread—some of the Bible commentaries seek to spiritualize this particular petition, and try to make it mean the same thing as Jesus meant when He said, "I am the bread of life . . ." (JOHN 6:35). These words can be taken literally, and can be applied to the actual physical needs of our life. We do have souls; but we also have physical bodies, and those physical bodies must be maintained. We have every right to ask our heavenly Father for the material needs of our lives. It is not wrong for me to ask God to help me make my business succeed, or to help me get a raise in my pay. God understands when we are burdened by debts and by the lack of things that we really need. I would hate to think that my children ever reached the place that they hesitated to talk with me about the physical needs of their lives, and our heavenly Father is just as concerned with His children.

At this point, it is well to note the pronouns that Jesus uses in this prayer: "our father"—"our daily bread"— "our trespasses"—"lead us not into temptation." We are taught here that our prayers can never involve just ourselves alone. We cannot really pray unless we include our fellow men. In prayer, we recognize our membership in the family of God. Lloyd C. Douglas said it beautifully in *The Big Fisherman:* "My own opinion of the mysterious Nazarene is difficult to define. On first sight of Him, I was a bit disappointed. He is not an heroic figure, but the man has a compelling voice. I can't describe it or the effect of it. It is a unifying voice that converts a great crowd of mutually distrustful strangers into a tight little group of blood relatives."

And forgive us our debts [*sins, trespasses*], *as we forgive our debtors* [*those who trespass against us*]—as we think of God, His glory, His goodness, His greatness; as we think of His Kingdom on earth, and His perfect will; as we think of our complete dependence upon Him, then naturally we come to confession. "Forgive us" comes readily to our lips. We think of where we have missed the Way. We think of the positive wrongs we have done. In His presence, we want no stains on our lives, no sins in our hearts. Having the Spirit of God firmly implanted in our consciousness as we have been praying to this point, we become more sure of God's willingness to forgive.

Many years ago, I heard an evangelist tell the story of a boy he saw riding on a train one day. The boy kept looking out the window and nervously rolling the brim of his hat. The preacher asked him what the trouble was, and the boy told him how he had run away from home, vowing he would never go back. But the world did not welcome him as he thought it would. He couldn't find a job, and he ran out of money. In desperation he wrote his father, asking if he would be welcome back home. His home was on the outskirts of a little town, and the boy said that he would be passing through on the train on a certain day, and that, if he were welcome at home, would his father please hang a towel on the front gate. If there were no towel, then the boy would not get off the train and would go on. As they neared the little town, the boy said to the preacher, "You look. I'm afraid to." The preacher looked out and saw not only a towel hanging on the post, but towels and sheets waving from the limbs of all the trees! He told the boy to look for himself. When the boy saw the welcome signs, he grabbed his old suitcase, put it under his arm, jumped off the train before it stopped, and ran down the dusty road toward his father's welcome.

We are so conscious and ashamed of our sins. But when we think of God and see Him, we are ready and eager to rush back into His arms.

. . . *as we forgive those who trespass against us*—recognizing our own need of forgiveness, and wanting a restored fellowship with the heavenly Father, it becomes easier to forgive those who have done us wrong. One of the most helpful experiences in prayer is to substitute the name of a particular person in this petition: "Forgive me as I forgive _____." As I pray this prayer, a name comes before me. Let me keep praying until that name is clear in my own mind and in my own heart.

And lead us not into temptation, but deliver us from evil—this is a recognition of our own weakness. Many people think of all the bad things that might happen, and worry about what they would do if those things should happen. When we think of sorrows, reverses, illnesses, and all the tragedies of life, we worry that we will not have strength to stand before them. So often, when some heavy burden falls upon us, we find that we have strength we did not know we had, and we can "walk through the valley."

Curiously, when we think of temptations and wrongs that might confront us, we have confidence to feel that we can handle them, and that we can walk with temptation without being hurt. Often it happens, when the temptation comes, that we discover weaknesses we did not know we had. So it is that trials bring out our strengths, and temptations uncover our weaknesses.

As we contemplate God and His strength, we become aware of our own inabilities, and we recognize our need for His help. Having been forgiven, we do not want to sin again. This is a prayer not only for strength in time of temptation, but also for escape from temptation. It is as John Ruskin expressed it: "No one can ask honestly or happily to be delivered from temptation unless he has honestly and firmly determined to do the best he can to keep out of it." Furthermore, this is a prayer that we may never become a temptation to someone else. In *Measure for Measure*, Shakespeare asked a very searching question: "The temptor or the tempted, who sins most?" Here is a question that can well occupy our minds.

For thine is the kingdom, and the power, and the glory, for ever—in some of the manuscripts, this phrase is omitted, but what a grand climax it is to the prayer! It ends our prayer where we began—centered in God. It is right and proper to pray for our own needs—for guidance, bread, forgiveness, strength—but our needs are never the beginning or the end. The glory belongs to

God. We never pray with only our own good in mind. *Thine is the kingdom* means that I accord to the King my disciplined obedience. *Thine is the power* means that I am not afraid, because God is able and sufficient in every situation. *Thine is the glory* means that I am not seeking glory for myself. *For ever* means that my horizon is lifted even beyond the bounds of time, and I know that God is for eternity.

Amen—this is one of the most important petitions of any prayer. We recall that when our Lord was hanging from the cross, He lifted His eyes and said, "Father, into thy hands I commend my spirit . . ." (LUKE 23:46). He had now given His best, and He was willing to entrust it all to the hands of God. The word "amen" means "faith in God"; it means a willingness to trust His willingness and His judgment and His power. The word "amen" brings to one a sense of deep confidence and relief.

Forgiving Others

For if ye forgive men their trespasses, your heavenly Father will also forgive you:

But if ye forgive not men their trespasses, neither will your Father forgive your trespasses (MATTHEW 6:14-15).

After Jesus had finished the Lord's Prayer, He felt it necessary to go back and lift out one of the petitions and give to it special emphasis: *. . . as we forgive our debtors.* In this connection, nearly all of us can think of some person we find difficult to forgive—someone who has done us an injustice. Sometimes we say, "I can forgive, but I cannot forget." Of course, we cannot wipe out our memories; and the truth is, forgiving at times will heighten recollection. But often by that expression we mean that we are unwilling to forget and that there are qualifications in our forgiveness.

Someone has told of a man who was on his death bed. He called an old enemy in to see him and said to him, "I want to forgive you for the wrong you did to me." But then he added, "but remember, if I get well, the old quarrel stands." Abe Martin, the old Indiana philosopher, once said, "Nobody ever forgets where he buried a hatchet." To forgive means that we quit harboring an injury in our minds; and it is amazing how a wrong can fade away if we stop thinking about it.

Also, let us remember that it is just as wrong to forget and not to forgive. Sometimes we can get tired of carrying old resentments, and just let them pass out of our minds. But, in truth, many times they do not really pass out of our minds. It may be that they are like an infection, becoming healed over the surface with the infection remaining in the body. We do need to forgive before we forget.

There is the story that Edwin Markham held in his heart a grudge against a banker who had violated his trust and left him penniless. After that experience, the poet could not write any more poetry. He would sit at his desk for long periods of time, trying to write but unable to make anything come out. Unconsciously, while he sat there, he was drawing circles on the sheet of paper instead of writing poetry. Then the thought came to him: "I've got to forgive him, or I shall die!" Looking at the circles which his subconscious mind had urged him to draw on the paper, he thought of the great encircling, forgiving love of God, and then said aloud, "I forgive him!" Then he wrote:

He drew a circle that shut me out—
Heretic, rebel, a thing to flout.
But Love and I had the wit to win:
We drew a circle that took him in.

With the resentment washed out of his soul, Markham began to write again, and during the next twenty years penned his masterpieces.

Refusing to forgive can do so much harm to any person. It can wreck his personal health, destroy his sense of well-being, spoil his relationship to other people. Most importantly, lack of forgiveness cuts him off from God. In truth, if we do not forgive others, God cannot forgive us.

In one of his sermons, Dr. Frank A. Court included this beautiful paragraph: "Forgiveness means the restoration of something precious that has been broken. It means the discovering once again of something beautiful that has been lost. It means knowing again a love that somehow has been broken. It is the reunion of that which life has allowed to become disjointed. It is harmony once again out of life's discord. It is the joy of companionship, once again, out of life's loneliness. It is life out of something sacred that we have allowed to die. It is faith and trust where there has been doubt, suspicion, and distrust. Yes, it is life's most beautiful word, and it has never been more beautiful than from the lips of Christ, 'Father, forgive them; for, they know not what they do.' "

When I see my Lord on the cross, and hear Him praying for the forgiveness of those who put Him there, I, too, can forgive.

Fasting

*Moreover when ye fast, be not, as the hypocrites, of a
sad countenance: for they disfigure their faces, that they
may appear unto men to fast. Verily I say unto you,
They have their reward.*

*But thou, when thou fastest, anoint thine head, and
wash thy face;*

*That thou appear not unto men to fast, but unto thy
Father which is in secret: and thy Father, which seeth in
secret, shall reward thee openly* (MATTHEW 6:16-18).

Along with giving and praying, fasting was one of the
really important religious acts of the people in Jesus' day.
It was compulsory that they were to fast on the day of
atonement. Also, they would fast at other times, such as
when they were in mourning, or when they were repent-
ing for some sin. Also, they would fast at times when
they were seeking some definite revelation from God.
We remember how Moses, when he was on the mountain
waiting for God to give him the Ten Commandments,
fasted for forty days and forty nights (EXODUS 24:18).

In our churches today, we do not hear *fasting* mentioned nearly as much as we hear *giving* and *praying*.
However, right now, across America, exercise and diet-
ing have become great fads, and almost a religion for a
lot of people. Many people are fasting to some degree for
health reasons. I read the other day of a woman com-
plaining to her doctor that her husband would not eat the
salads and vegetables she prepared for him, and that he
called them "rabbit food." The doctor replied to the
woman, "Tell your husband that it may be rabbit food,

but never forget that a middle-aged rabbit doesn't have an over-sized stomach; he still has his own teeth, hasn't lost his romantic appeal to other rabbits, and can still run as fast as when he was young."

Fasting in many instances is good for our physical bodies, but there are times when it can be good for our souls. In his commentary on Matthew, Dr. William Barclay lists a number of good reasons for fasting: (1) It is good for health; (2) it is good for self-discipline; (3) it preserves us from becoming slaves of a habit; (4) it preserves the ability to do without things; (5) it makes us appreciate things all the more.

Maybe it would be good to re-emphasize the importance of fasting in our day and generation. But, again, our Lord warns that even the fine experience of fasting can be ruined by the wrong motives. When one fasts merely to impress other people, then it is of no value. That was the danger in Jesus' day. Certain of the hypocrites (actors) put on a *sad countenance: for they disfigure their faces, that they may appear unto men to fast.* And, many times, those people were seeking to say to those who saw them: "You see how good I am. I do not need to fast for myself, but there are so many people who do need it that I am doing this for them." For many of those people, fasting became a sign of superior piety, and all of the value of it was destroyed.

The other night I was at a meeting until about nine o'clock. After the meeting I drove by the hospital to see a little girl who was very sick. Sitting by her bedside was her mother. I asked the mother, "Did you have any supper?"

She replied, "No."

I said, "Did you eat any lunch?"

She replied, "No." She looked up at me and said, "I

have been so concerned about little Ruth that I have not wanted anything to eat."

It is possible for one's mind to be so firmly fixed on God that he just does not care for physical food. In that instance, the fasting comes from the heart and from the soul, and it becomes a blessed experience.

Treasures in Heaven

Lay not up for yourselves treasures upon earth, where moth and rust doth corrupt, and where thieves break through and steal:

But lay up for yourselves treasures in heaven, where neither moth nor rust doth corrupt, and where thieves do not break through nor steal:

For where your treasure is, there will your heart be also (MATTHEW 6:19-21).

Here is a passage in which modern Americans lose interest from the very first sentence: "Lay not up for yourselves treasures upon earth. . . ." The typical American success story is entitled "From Rags to Riches"—the way to make your mark in the world through hard work, perseverance, thrift, and brains. Horatio Alger is still our national hero in one form or another. Talk to parents and you will find that most hope their children will make a greater success in life than they have. We want our children to have a better education, better opportunities, to live in better houses, and make more money. But we do not think too much of our children's developing a finer character than we have. Our idea of success in life is determined by the treasures we lay up here upon earth.

According to our standards of success, Jesus was one

of the failures of history. He disappointed His friends and followers. His family considered Him a hopeless dreamer. He was trained for a respectable trade but turned His back upon it. He never drew a salary, never saved any money, never even owned a house in which to live. He achieved none of the status symbols that we consider so important—a flashy new car, two television sets, an honorary degree, and so on. The only status symbol He achieved was a cross on which He suffered a lonely death. What a tragedy for such a fine young Man to come to such a dreary end! Today we call Him "Lord," but multitudes of us do not really worship the kind of success that He achieved.

Nevertheless, He warns us against "treasures upon earth, where moth and rust doth corrupt, and where thieves break through and steal." The moth can destroy cloth, and cloth is what clothes are made of. The word translated "rust" literally means an "eating away"; it may refer to metals, it may refer to wood that can decay, it may refer to food such as corn and grain stored away where rats and worms and other vermin can eat it. Or one may hoard up certain treasures in his house, and one day come home to find that thieves have broken in and carried his treasures away. The thing our Lord is warning against is the giving of our lives for those things which are only temporary.

Once a rich man in the community died, and someone asked, "How much did he leave?"

Another replied, "He left all he had."

There is the tragedy of so many lives. We forget that the supreme effort of life here is the preparation for the life hereafter. It is true that we should want to live, but we also need to remember that there is a vast difference between living today and living *for* today. There is a story that St. Philip of Neri questioned his students who came to study law; he would ask, "Why did you come?"

The student would answer, "To study law."

"What will you do when you have studied the law?"

"I will set up an office and practice."

"What then?"

"I will get married and have a family."

"What then?"

"I will enjoy my home and my work."

"What then?"

"I will grow older."

"What then?"

"I will retire."

"What then?"

"I will eventually die."

Thus, the great teacher forced the student to recognize the need for doing more than merely preparing for this life. Our destiny is not to be found in one world, but in two.

Once a man was visiting a great art gallery. Nearby he saw a woman on her knees, scrubbing the floor. He turned to her and said, "There are many beautiful paintings here." She replied, "I suppose so, if a body has the time to look up." There is the tragedy: we become so engrossed in this world that we do not ever take the time or have the inclination to look up.

Life here on this earth is such a real experience that there is a danger that the reality of this life may overshadow in our mind the reality of the next life. We constantly need to remind ourselves of the fact—and we must emphasize the word "fact"—of the life beyond.

Cecil B. DeMille told this wonderful experience: "Many years ago, I was commissioned by David Belasco to write a play, *The Return of Peter Grimm*. The play was being written for David Warfield, and the story hinged upon the continuation of life after death.

"I got the inspiration for that story from a water beetle. I was up on a lake in the Main woods. The canoe was drifting. I was reading-resting-searching for an idea. I looked down in the water, for my little craft had drifted to where the lake was only about four inches deep. There in a world of mud and wet, were water beetles. One crawled up on the gunwale, stuck the talons on his legs into the woodwork and died.

"I let it alone and turned to my reading. The sun was hot. In about three hours I looked at my water beetle again. He was parched. His back was cracking open. I watched and out of the back of that dead beetle I saw crawling a new form—a moist head—then wings. A most beautiful dragonfly. It scintillated all the colors of the rainbow.

"As I sat watching, it flew farther in a second than the water beetle had crawled in days. It hovered above the surface, just a few inches from the water beetles beneath. They did not know it was there.

"I took my fingertip and moved the shriveled water beetle husk from the canoe's gunwale. It fell back into the lake and sank down to the mud-covered bottom. The other water beetles crawled awkwardly to see what it was. It was a dead body. They backed away from it.

"If God does that for a water beetle, don't you believe He will do it for me."

We "lay up treasures in heaven" as we live for God, as we invest in deeds of love, in acts of forgiveness and understanding. We become rich toward God as we turn our backs on deeds that are wrong and shoddy and cheap; and as we take our place in the service of life, we make deposits in the bank of heaven when we live with hope, courage, faith, and love; and as we trust God with the explanations which we cannot now understand. When we live in loyal obedience to Christ, we accumulate wealth that will outlast this earth. The Bible teaches us that even a cup of water given in His name will draw rich dividends.

Let us remind ourselves that we do not have to wait for death to enjoy much of our heavenly wealth. A clear conscience brings more satisfaction than money in the bank. Satisfaction in a life well lived is a great reward, and the faith to face the future unafraid is true wealth. When Edwin Markham was past eighty years of age, he had so lived that he could write:

> I have bidden the past adieu.
> I laugh and lift hand to the years ahead:
> "Come on: I am ready for you!"

When one has laid up "treasure in heaven," the present is a happy experience and the future holds no fear.

All of us can call to mind certain ones we have known who became heavenly rich. Across the years, two of the people I have loved the most are Bishop and Mrs. Arthur J. Moore. After Mrs. Moore's death, I received a letter from Bishop Moore, which I cherish dearly. He wrote:

"My dearly beloved Martha walked triumphantly into God's house on Monday, August 17th. You can imagine how lonely the children and I feel.

"For more than fifty-eight years, her unfaltering faith, her compassionate heart and wise judgments have been for me an unfailing source of inspiration and courage. She was a woman of rare gifts, unfailing in her fidelity to her Master, her family and to an innumerable company of friends, who stretch literally around the earth.

"We who walked close by her side can never cease to be grateful for her radiant singing soul and Christlike compassion.

"In these months of serious illness, her brave beauty and victorious faith were as clear as sunlight. In her final written word to those she loved best, she said, 'I neither fear death, nor dread to die.' In this earthly life she lived in God, now in that land where shadows never darken she lives with God. In life she held 'her own' securely in her love. Now that she is away for a little while, we shall hold her forever in our undying affection and loving memory.

"We of the family will strive to walk with larger hope and braver step until we greet her in the morning of the fadeless day."

Truly, Mrs. Arthur Moore knew the meaning of heavenly wealth.

Heaven is very real. I would like to close this section with one of the loveliest stories I have ever read. I do not know the source, but here it is:

In October of 1800, a boy named John Todd was born in Rutland, Vermont. Shortly afterward, the family moved to the little village of Killingsworth. And there, when John was only six years of age, both his parents died. The children in the home had to be parceled out among the relatives, and a kind-hearted aunt who lived in North Killingsworth agreed to take John and give him a home. With her he lived until some fifteen years later when he went away to study for the ministry. When he was in middle life, his aunt fell desperately ill and realized that death could not be far off. In great distress, she wrote her nephew a pitiful letter—what would death be like? Would it mean the end of everything, or would there be, beyond death, a chance to continue living, growing, loving? Here is the letter John Todd sent in reply:

"It is now thirty-five years since I, a little boy of six, was left quite alone in the world. You sent me word you would give me a home and be a kind mother to me. I have never forgotten the day when I made the long journey of ten miles to your house in North Killingsworth. I can still recall my disappointment when, instead of coming for me yourself, you sent your colored man, Caesar, to fetch me. I well remember my tears and my anxiety as, perched high on your horse and clinging tight to Caesar, I rode off to my new home. Night fell before we finished the journey and as it grew dark, I became lonely and afraid.

" 'Do you think she'll go to bed before I get there?' I asked Caesar, anxiously.

" 'O no,' he said, reassuringly. 'She'll sure stay up *for you*. When we get out of these here woods, you'll see her candle shining in the window.'

"Presently we did ride out in the clearing and there, sure enough, was your candle. I remember you were waiting at the door, that you put your arms close about me and that you lifted me—a tired and bewildered little boy—down from the horse. You had a big fire burning on the hearth, a hot supper waiting for me on the stove. After supper, you took me to my new room, you heard me say my prayers and then you sat beside me until I fell asleep.

"You probably realized why I am recalling all this to your memory. Some day soon, God will send for you, to take you to a new home. Don't fear the summons—the strange journey—or the dark messenger of death. God can be trusted to do as much for you as you were kind enough to do for me so many years ago. At the end of the road you will find love and a welcome waiting, and you will be safe in God's care. I shall watch you and pray for you until you are out of sight and then wait for the day when I shall make the journey myself and find you waiting at the end of the road to greet me.

"This is the Christian's faith. Behind and beneath life it sees God's unfailing love. Beyond death it confidently expects the new opportunities which a kind Father can be trusted to provide for all his children."

The Single Eye

The light of the body is the eye: if therefore thine eye be single, thy whole body shall be full of light.

But if thine eye be evil, thy whole body shall be full of darkness. If therefore the light that is in thee be darkness, how great is that darkness (MATTHEW 6:22-23).

A man who was planning a visit to New York asked a friend of his who knew the city well to tell him what kind of a city New York really is. The friend told him that New York is both the best city in America and the worst city; he told him it would depend on what he looked for. In New York he could find some of the most beautiful churches in the world. He could hear some of the greatest preachers. He could see in the art galleries some of the most beautiful paintings. He could hear some of the world's most glorious music played there. He could attend some of the finest dramatic productions the world affords. He could eat in some of the nicest restaurants. Indeed, if he looked for it, he could find in New York the good and the beautiful and the true.

On the other hand, in that same city, he could find some

of the worst slums. He could see some of the most hardened criminals. He could visit some of the cheapest and the most vulgar honkey-tonks. There, he could associate with people who had sunk to the lowest level of life in every respect. If he wanted to look for it, he could find New York to be the very worst city there is. So, whether his visit to New York was to be one of joy and inspiration, or one of despair and discouragement, was dependent upon what he looked for.

The same may be said of the very places in which we live. Up and down our own streets, we can see people with neighborly spirits and loving hearts. Or we can see pettiness and dirt in the lives of our neighbors. Our attitudes toward our fellow men are determined not by what people are, but by what we see in them. Or the same is true even in an individual. We can see the good, the true, in every person, or we can see his faults and his shortcomings. If we have an eye out for the good, then the good comes within our lives: ". . . thy whole body shall be full of light." But if we are always looking for the evil, then the darkness comes within our lives: ". . . thy whole body shall be full of darkness."

In this connection, the words of Proverbs 4:23 come alive for us: "Keep thy heart with all diligence; for out of it are the issues of life." That is, the things we admit into our hearts determine our lives. If one is to build a life of health, happiness, and abundance, he must concentrate on love, light, beauty, truth, and peace, and all of the attributes of God. As Jesus speaks here of the "single eye," He is saying what St. Paul said: "Finally, brethren, whatsoever things are true, whatsoever things are honest, whatsoever things are just, whatsoever things are pure, whatsoever things are lovely, whatsoever things are of good report; if there be any virtue, and if there be any praise, think on these things" (PHILIPPIANS 4:8).

On the other hand, if you think hatred, jealousy, lust, anger, failure, prejudice, self-conceit, and such things, then your whole life will be filled with darkness.

In *The Family Reunion* T. S. Eliot has Harry saying, "I feel quite happy, as if happiness did not consist in getting what one wanted or in getting rid of what can't be got rid of, but in a different vision." That is, one finds happiness not by changing his or her circumstances, but in taking a different view of life.

> The night has a thousand eyes,
> And the day but one;
> Yet the light of the bright world dies
> With the dying sun.
>
> The mind has a thousand eyes,
> And the heart but one;
> Yet the light of a whole life dies
> When love is done.
>
> "Light," Francis W. Bourdillon

The great tragedy in the lives of so many people is that they have eyes, but do not really see. Helen Keller was blind from the time she was a baby, yet through life she has seen the true beauties and wonders. Once she said, "I have walked with people whose eyes are full of light but who see nothing in sea or sky, nothing in city streets, nothing in books. It were far better to sail forever in the night of blindness with sense, and feelings, and mind, than to be content with the mere act of seeing. The only lightless dark is the night of darkness in ignorance and insensibility."

There is another interpretation of this passage which Moffatt gives us. He translates these words to read: ". . . if your Eye is generous, the whole of your body will be illumined, but if your Eye is selfish, the whole of your body will be darkened."

If a person is looking for and seeing opportunities to serve God and his fellow men—maybe through the gift of some material thing, or a kind and encouraging word, or an expression of love and interest—through giving of himself to others, light comes into his own life. On the other hand, if one closes his eyes to all the opportunities for service around him, gradually darkness pervades his very soul and the light of his life goes out.

Two Masters

No man can serve two masters: for either he will hate the one, and love the other; or else he will hold to the one, and despise the other. Ye cannot serve God and mammon (MATTHEW 6:24).

Here Jesus was using a well-understood situation in the society of His day to point out an eternal truth in reference to the Kingdom of God.

First, let us see clearly the situation to which He was referring. In that day, slavery was a common practice, and a slave had absolutely no individual rights of his own. The slave's master had absolute authority over him, including every single moment of the slave's time. The slave was on duty at all hours. In our society we have a practice which we call "moonlighting"; by that, we mean a man can hold down two jobs at once. A man may give, say, forty hours a week to one job, and then in his "off" hours do some other work. But that was impossible for slaves of Jesus' day. The slave had no off hours; therefore, he could not be the slave of two masters. He belonged entirely to one master.

We have the same principle in our marriages today. In the marriage ceremony, the minister includes in the vows to both the bride and the groom these words: "And forsaking all others, keep thee only unto her (or, him) so long as ye both shall live." Suppose John at that time answered, "Yes, I love Mary, whom I am now marrying, but I also love Susan and Elizabeth and Margaret. Now, I intend to be loyal to Mary and make her a good husband, but I do not want to cut my romantic ties with others that I have learned to love. I want to be free to spend some time with these others and enjoy their fellowship and their love." A marriage based on that principle would never work. A happy marriage is based on the fundamental that each one gives himself or herself completely and entirely to the other. "You cannot be married to two people."

Likewise, Jesus says that we have to make an absolute decision between God and mammon. If we choose God, He must be the undisputed Master of our lives. The godly person is one who has no time of his own. He cannot say, "I will serve God during these hours; but, in my off hours, I will do as I please." There are no off hours in our service to God. We belong to him all of the time—while we are at work, at play, at home, and wherever we may be. The principle here is that one must make a definite and complete decision.

I am sure that there is no person who pleases God less than the one who cannot make up his mind. Read again these condemning words which the Spirit of God directed St. John to write to the church of Laodicea: "I know thy works, that thou art neither cold nor hot: I would thou wert cold or hot. So then, because thou art lukewarm, and neither cold nor hot, I will spew thee out of my mouth" (REVELATION 3:15-16). This is indeed strong language; for the one who cannot determine which side he is on, the Lord says He will "vomit him up."

I am sure that indecision is one, if not the, most harmful experience in the life of any person—harmful, first, because it squanders his energies. I still remember an experience that I had as a little boy. Several of us were playing in the pasture down by the side of the creek. We got to talking about whether or not any one of us could jump over the creek. I looked at the creek and said I believed I could do it. And the other boys dared me to try. I got back a distance, so as to get a good running start. As I was getting close to the creek, however, it looked wider and wider, and I began to have some doubt that I could do it. I started to jump at the same time I felt that I ought to have held back. The result was that I landed in the middle of the creek! I got all wet and was laughed at by my friends. If I had resolutely made up my mind to jump the creek, I believe I could have done it. My indecision squandered my power.

One of the most tragic airplane accidents in history took place in France several years ago. One who was at the airport and saw it told me that the heavily-loaded plane started down the runway. It was gathering speed but not as fast as it should have. After the plane got a considerable distance down the runway, the pilot decided he would try to stop it, but he was going too fast to stop and the result was a crash in which many lives were lost.

My friend who saw the accident said that he believed that if the pilot had kept his motors open and continued to go on, he would have gathered enough speed to take off safely. The crash came because of his indecision.

One thinks of St. Paul when he said, ". . . this one thing I do . . ." (PHILIPPIANS 3:13). When one focuses all his powers upon a single object, he discovers strength that he never knew he had. But when one cannot decide, then his life becomes weakened and possibly even paralyzed.

I remember a cartoon that I saw, a picture of a donkey standing between two haystacks. The donkey was hungry and the aroma of the hay was appetizing. He would look toward one haystack and start; then he would think of the other haystack, and look back, and start toward it. The end of the cartoon was that the poor donkey starved to death, standing between the two fragrant haystacks, simply because he never could make up his mind.

This was the trouble with Hamlet. Hamlet did not have the ability to act, and so he said, "To be, or not to be, that is the question." He never could decide.

One thinks of Pilate. Pilate had nothing against Jesus, and he did not care to condemn Him. I feel sure that Pilate even admired Jesus. On the other hand the crowd was shouting at him, and there was the danger that he might be accused of not being Caesar's friend. So Pilate could not decide to let Jesus go or to crucify Him. Instead, he sought to "wash his hands" of the entire affair. But, in not taking a stand, Pilate took the wrong stand, and his name has been written in infamy down through the centuries.

One remembers the words of the prophet Elijah as he said to the people, "How long halt ye between two opinions? if the Lord be God, follow him: but if Baal, then follow him" (I KINGS 18:21).

It is said that when Robert Louis Stevenson had an important decision to make, he would write in one column all of the reasons why he should do that certain thing. Then, in another column, he would write down all the reasons why he should not do it. He would compare the two columns he had written, and make his decision. Suppose we faced up to our decision with Christ in this way? Put down in one column all of the reasons why you believe that following Christ is in the best interests of your life. Then, in the other column, put down why you believe that rejecting Christ would bring you a better life. Then study the two columns, and make up your mind. The great misfortune of so many people today is that they never really face up to the decision.

Jesus said, *Ye cannot serve God and mammon*. Mammon was a Hebrew word meaning "material things." There comes the time in our lives when we have to decide between possessing God and the possessions of this life.

On one occasion, Jesus said, "Remember Lot's wife" (LUKE 17:32). She is a perfect example of indecision. Being the member of a family which gave us our greatest prophets and purest saints, there was within her the faith of her family. She knew God, and from her childhood had known the meaning of prayer. But, along with her husband, she had moved into Sodom, the city of mammon. More importantly, Sodom had moved into her: she wanted God, but she also wanted Sodom. Finally, the day of decision came. She made a start toward God, but she looked back toward Sodom. Reaching for the stars with one hand and fingering the mud with the other, she revealed her divided heart which brought misery and eventual destruction.

What is the most complete picture of restlessness to be

seen? I think it is the sea. Ceaselessly the ocean rises and falls back again. It can never be still. The voice of the sky is constantly calling to it. The ocean is drawn upon by magnet in the heavens, but the muddy old world holds on and demands, "Stay with me." The ocean can never completely decide, and neither can it stop its ears to the voices from the earth and from the heavens. Thus, it is always tossing, and never finds peace and rest.

So it is with man. Within each of us there are two forces struggling to become our master. One is our ideals, the call of the holy life, the desire to be good and godly. The other is our selfish desire, our worldly nature. Goethe said, "It is regrettable that nature made only one man when there is material aplenty for both a rogue and a gentleman." We may choose the low life, but even then we will not have peace, because God never leaves us alone. It is as Augustine said: "Man is restless until he finds his rest in Thee, O God."

Consider the picture of our Lord when "he stedfastly set his face to go to Jerusalem" (LUKE 9:51). He heard the voice of inclination, and He also heard the voice of God. He made up His mind; there was no wavering. After making His complete decision, we all know that our Lord found both courage and calmness. He was never really afraid. Even as He hung upon the pain-drenched cross, He spoke a calm valedictory: "Father, into thy hands I commend my spirit . . ." (LUKE 23:46).

We must settle this matter of who is our master before we can really know what our Lord is talking about in the next passage of the Sermon on the Mount.

Overcoming Your Anxiety

Therefore I say unto you, Take no thought for your life, what ye shall eat, or what ye shall drink; nor yet for your body, what ye shall put on. Is not the life more than meat, and the body than raiment?

Behold the fowls of the air: for they sow not, neither do they reap, nor gather into barns; yet your heavenly Father feedeth them. Are ye not much better than they?

Which of you by taking thought can add one cubit unto his stature?

And why take ye thought for raiment? Consider the lilies of the field, how they grow; they toil not, neither do they spin:

And yet I say unto you, That even Solomon in all his glory was not arrayed like one of these.

Wherefore, if God so clothe the grass of the field, which to day is, and to morrow is cast into the oven, shall he not much more clothe you, O ye of little faith?

Therefore take no thought, saying, What shall we eat? or, What shall we drink? or, Wherewithal shall we be clothed?

(For after all these things do the Gentiles seek:) for your heavenly Father knoweth that ye have need of all these things.

But seek ye first the kingdom of God, and his righteousness; and all these things shall be added unto you.

Take therefore no thought for the morrow: for the morrow shall take thought for the things of itself. Sufficient unto the day is the evil thereof (MATTHEW 6:25-34).

Take no thought for your life . . .—the expresssion "take thought" comes out of seventeenth-century English; it meant, "Do not be anxious or worried." Jesus specifically mentioned that we should not worry about food and drink and clothes, meaning the material essentials of life. This does not mean that Jesus was indifferent to our physical needs. Look at His own life. The scholars tell us that Joseph died when Jesus was but a Youth, and that the burden of supporting His dear mother and brothers and sisters fell upon His shoulders. In that day, providing food and clothing was no easy matter. He knew the struggles that ordinary people had to face. Later in His ministry, He talked about such things as putting leaven in the meal, and a little boy's lunch of loaves and fishes. He talked about the patching of old garments, and a diligent searching for one small coin that had been lost in a house. One of the reasons that the "common people heard him gladly" was that He understood their lives.

Certainly Jesus never taught that we were not to make reasonable plans for the future. Because we do believe in the future, we want to prepare for it. That is why a student goes to school, or why one takes out an insurance policy, or opens a savings account, or makes a will. Because one does think of the future, he does not want to go into debt beyond his reasonable ability to pay. Jesus pointed out that one should not only love God with his heart and his soul, but, He also added, ". . . with all thy mind" (MATTHEW 22:37). He expected us to be reasonable people at all times, and one mark of a reasonable person is advance planning.

Jesus said, "For which of you, intending to build a tower, sitteth not down first, and counteth the cost, whether ye have sufficient to finish it?" (LUKE 14:28).

· *135*

Of the man who thought only of eating and drinking and being merry today, Jesus said, "He is a fool" (see LUKE 12:16-20).

The *Revised Standard Version* translates these words: ". . . do not be anxious about your life. . . ." The word "anxious" has two meanings. First, it means desire; second, it means fear. One type of anxiety leads to careful planning and preparation. The other one leads to morbid worry. One is good; the other is very harmful.

However, there is still a third type of worry or anxiety that we need to consider also. The novelist E. M. Forster made this observation: "One has two duties—to be worried and not to be worried." When he talked about the "duty" to be worried, he was talking about our society and our obligations to it. He was talking about our duty to lay upon our hearts and our consciences the needs of mankind. Remember how William Lloyd Garrison took his share of the burden and pain borne by his Negro brethren. He "saw in the sorrowful face of the slave the shattered face of God."

Someone once asked Leslie Tizard how he received the call to the ministry. His reply was: "If I were asked how the call came to me, I should reply that it was through the sense of human needs. There was a transport strike in London and I was walking through a drab street in the East End as the crowds were turning out of the beer parlors. A drunken man reeled across the path in front of me and fell like a log in the middle of the road. There was no roar of traffic that night to drown the sickening helpless thud of his fall. I could hear it for months afterwards. It symbolized for me the helplessness of foolish and sinful men for which there was no cure apart from God. I knew then how much men needed the Gospel, and for the first time offered my life for the preaching of it."

One is reminded of Isaiah's experience when he walked into the temple and saw God. As he looked into the face of God he saw the uncleanness of his own soul. Also he recognized the fact that he lived in a world where there were unclean men, and he heard the voice of the Lord saying, "Whom shall I send, and who will go for us?" Isaiah replied, "Here am I; send me" (ISAIAH 6:1-8).

When the Christian sees human need, he has a duty to be worried about it—worried to the point that he gives himself in doing something about it. The Christian is never unconcerned.

Let us put our ability to be anxious to a good purpose. Let us learn to be anxious about the schools in our community, about the recreational programs for youth, about the environment of our home, about the condition of our churches. It would be a very helpful exercise for any Christian to make a list of the things that he feels Christ would like for him to be anxious about, with his anxiety leading him to some positive action. Christians need to be anxious, but, as our Lord points out, not about their own affairs, but about the things that matter most.

Live One Day at a Time

In regard to the anxiety which leads to morbid worry and fear, Jesus did not content Himself with merely saying, "Do not be anxious." Instead, He gave us two ways to overcome this destructive anxiety: (1) He said we are to live one day at a time—"for the morrow shall take thought for the things of itself. Sufficient unto the day is the evil thereof." I like Moffatt's translation of these words: ". . . to-morrow will take care of itself. The day's own trouble is enough for the day." This simply means that we are to live one day at a time.

Sir William Ostler, the famous physician and one of the founders of Johns Hopkins University, tells of a night when he was almost worried sick; his final examination was coming up the next day. Beyond that, he was worried about the future. He picked up a copy of Carlyle's works and read this familiar sentence: "Our main business is not to see what lies dimly at a distance, but to do what lies clearly at hand." Years later, when Dr. Ostler returned to his native England to be knighted by the king, he said; "more than anything else I owe whatever success I have had to the power of settling down to the day's work and trying to do it to the best of my ability, and letting the future take care of itself."

Robert Wuillen told of a famous old naturalist who began to cut trees to build a log house. A friend said to him, "Isn't that a big undertaking for a man of your years?"

He replied, "It would be if I thought of chopping the trees, sawing the logs, skinning the bark, laying the foundation, erecting the walls, and putting on the roof. Carrying the load all at once would exhaust me. But it isn't so hard to cut down this one tree, and that is all I have to do now."

Someone told of walking into the kitchen after supper one night and seeing his wife washing dishes. He thought to himself: "If that poor woman could just look ahead and see the dishes that will remain to be washed in the future, towering like a mountain, she would give up right away." Then, he thought, "But she has only to wash today's dishes."

First, one of the difficulties in living today is that we

are burdened by our old decisions of yesterday. Where is there one among us who has not said, "If I had only made a different decision, my life would be better now"? Suppose you had married some other person, or entered some other line of work, or settled in some other city? One help at this point is to remind yourself that you do not know the road you did not take. In your imagination you think of that other road as being smooth and straight and leading directly to your heart's desire, but you cannot be sure. That other road may have been more wearisome and more heartbreaking. A second help is to remind yourself that you have not yet seen all of the road which you did choose. Maybe you are having hardships and difficulties now, but who knows—tomorrow may bring a turning point; if not tomorrow, maybe next week, or next month, or next year. It is just possible that on the road you are now traveling, you will run head-on into happiness, the happiness you had begun to think was on the road you did not choose.

One day, Lloyd George and a friend of his were walking across a field. As they walked, his friend asked Lloyd George how he had been able to keep his inner composure and strength during the difficult days of the First World War. As they came to the end of the field, Mr. George opened the gate, and after they had walked through, he carefully closed it. Then he said, "Right here is my secret. I always close the gate behind me and concentrate on where I am walking now." In order to be able to give our best to the present, we must be able to close the gates of the past.

Second, we must realize that many of the hardships and unhappinesses of today are not permanent. Someone once asked an old retired minister what his favorite Bible verse was. Quickly came his reply: "And it came to

· *139*

pass." He went on to explain that through a long life he had come to realize that the heartaches, troubles, wars, debts, and all the burdens of mankind "come to pass." One remembers the words spoken to Job: ". . . thou shalt forget thy misery, and remember it as waters that pass away" (JOB 11:16).

This same truth applies to the happy, delightful experiences of life as well. We need to learn to enjoy the joys of each day, because they too "come to pass." Wouldn't it be wonderful if we could keep that precious little child in our home, just as he is, so that one day, when we had time, we could play with him and enjoy him? But that little child doesn't stay the way he is. He has growing power, and if we expect to enjoy our child, we have to enjoy him when we have the opportunity.

In reference to both our burdens and our pleasures, let us remember that they do "come to pass." Knowing that truth, we can face them squarely day by day.

Third, in living one day at a time, we must not try to run ahead into tomorrow. Isn't it true that most of our worries are borrowed from tomorrow? We worry about mountains we may never have to climb, about streams we may never have to cross, about enemies we may never have to face. It has been pointed out that Lloyd's of London has gotten rich by betting that what people worry about will never happen.

One assurance that helps us to overcome our fears for tomorrow is the fact that we will be given the strength we need. We are promised in God's words: ". . . and as thy days, so shall thy strength be" (DEUTERONOMY 33:25); that is, we will have the strength we need when the time comes. Professor MacDougall in one of his books tells about a boy who was chased across a field by an infuriated bull. He succeeded in leaping over a high fence and saving himself. Sometime later, the boy went back to that fence and tried to jump it again. He made repeated efforts, but never could accomplish it, yet in his moment of great need he had had unusual strength.

What we do is to anticipate our needs in the future, and we try to match them with our present resources. We fail to consider that perhaps we will be stronger and more able when those needs arise. The Psalmist put it this way: "Thou preparest a table before me in the presence of mine enemies . . ." (PSALM 23:5). You are stronger than you think. You are braver than you think. Wait until the need arises before you begin to worry about it. So—Jesus said that one way to keep from being anxious about tomorrow is to concentrate on the living of today.

Thomas S. Kepler in one of his books tells about a group of 104 psychologists who made a study of their cases and determined a timetable for anxiety: At 18, we worry about ideals, at 20, we worry about appearance; at 23, about morals; at 26, about making a good impression; at 30, about salary and the cost of living; at 31, about business success; at 33, about job security; at 41, about politics; at 42, about marital problems; at 45, about the loss of ambition; over 45, about health. Most of our worries are useless.

As one puts his best into the living of each day, he goes a long way toward the elimination of his worries, fears, and anxieties.

Trust in God

In overcoming our anxieties, not only are we to live one day at a time, but our Lord said, "Take *therefore* no thought for the morrow. . . ." In our church conferences, we frequently hear resolutions. The resolution will state, "whereas" this, and "whereas" that, and "whereas" something else, setting forth certain facts and conditions. Then it will draw a conclusion: "therefore" we can and should do the following. In this passage our Lord lays down certain truths on which we can depend:

Behold the fowls of the air: . . . your heavenly Father feedeth them—I have an idea that Jesus was pointing to the little sparrows that were flying around when He referred to "fowls of the air." He might have said, "consider the eagle, the monarch of the sky," and He might have pointed out that God cares for the great, strong eagle. Or He might have said "Consider the nightingale, the one who charms us with its beautiful melody, reminding us of the singing of the angels." Sometimes it does seem that God grants special favors to those who are strongest and most talented. The little sparrows are insignificant little things, but those who are familiar with birds know that the sparrows are friendly and unafraid. We recall how our Lord pointed out that people could buy two sparrows in the marketplace for a penny, and yet never a sparrow fell to the ground without the heavenly Father knowing about it (MATTHEW 10:29). I think Jesus was saying here that God's care is extended to the most humble and least important of the birds. Then Jesus asked: "Are ye not much better than they?"

When you consider the worth of a human being, made in the image of God, in comparison to that of a sparrow; and when you consider God's care of the sparrow; therefore, is it not reasonable to assume that God will also care for His children? The poet sums it up beautifully in these words:

Said the robin to the sparrow,
I should really like to know
Why these anxious human beings
Rush around and worry so.

Said the sparrow to the robin,
Friend, I think that it must be
That they have no heavenly Father
Such as cares for you and me.

Then Jesus said, *Consider the lilies of the field, how they grow; . . . even Solomon in all his glory was not arrayed like one of these.* Again, Jesus was pointing out one of the humblest of God's creatures. He did not refer to some beautiful flower growing in a magnificent palace; instead it was a common little wildflower of the field. Suppose we talk to the little lily and seek to find out its secret: "Lily, Jesus said you are more glorious than Solomon. How did you attain your glory? Do you have a magic formula?"

"No," says the lily, "I simply grew."

"Then you were not always the glorious creature that you are now?"

The lily replies, "No, I once was a bulb. Then I was planted in the ground. Out of me a little green shoot came, and little by little I just grew. But I want you to know that I did not grow all by myself. I was planted in the soil that God provided. His sun warmed and lighted my way. He sent the gentle showers to give me moisture. And I breathed the air that He created. God took care of my every need."

If one listens to the lily, he may hear the lily saying, "There was a time when I resented the fact that I was nothing but a little lily. I looked at the sunflower, so tall and straight, and I wanted to be like that. Or I could see the great oak tree over yonder, and I thought about how long the tree would live, and I wanted to be a tree. But then I realized that God made me a lily, and that was all that I could be. So I set out to be the finest lily that I could be."

As we keep listening, we may hear the lily saying, "There is something else God taught me. When I first began to grow into a lily, I was very happy. Then the bees and the birds would come along and take some of my sweetness. The workers in the field would walk by and look upon me. The wind would steal some of my perfume. I began to be afraid that all I had would be gone. I felt as if I should veil my face and keep all I had, but when I did that, I began to wither and die. And then it was I learned that the fine art of living is the fine art of giving."

Then the lily might look at one of us and speak very seriously: "God has done all of this for me, and yet I am going to live for such a short time. You heard for yourself Jesus' words: 'Wherefore, if God so clothe the grass of the field, which to day is, and to morrow is cast into the oven, shall he not much more clothe you . . . ?" You are made in the likeness of God. You are His child. You can think God's thoughts after Him. You can render God's services. You are made with a soul that will live eternally; when your life is over, you will be with God in His house. When you look at me and realize how much God has done for me, just think about how much more He will do for you."

Jesus is saying to each one of us: "When you look about you in God's creation, and see what God has done for all of His creatures, and then consider how much more important a human being is, is it not reasonable to have faith and confidence in Him?"

A hundred years ago there lived in Georgia a brilliant young poet by the name of Sidney Lanier. He had youth and vigor and a love of life. He could look at the muddy, crooked Chattahoochee River and make it sing ("Song of the Chattahoochee"):

> Out of the hills of Habersham,
> Down the valleys of Hall,
> I hurry amain to reach the plain,
> Run the rapid and leap the fall.

When Sidney Lanier was in his mid-thirties, however, he developed tuberculosis. He knew he would not live—nobody in those days lived through that dread disease. He went down to Glenn County on the coast where the climate was milder. Sitting there one day, looking out across the marshes, he wrote his finest poem ("The Marshes of Glynn"), in which he said:

> As the march-hen secretly builds on the watery sod,
> Behold I will build me a nest on the greatness of God.

The second way we overcome our anxious fears is to build our faith in the God who knows us, who loves us, and who cares for us. Bishop William Quayle discovered for himself the meaning of Jesus' words. One night he could not sleep because he was so worried about a problem he was to face the coming day. He paced the floor of his bedroom long past midnight. Then he told about how, in the stillness of his own heart, he heard God say, "Quayle, you go back to bed. I'll sit up the rest of the night." Perhaps the Psalmist had had a similar experience

· *145*

which caused him to write: "It is vain for you to rise up early, to sit up late, to eat the bread of sorrows: for so he giveth His beloved sleep" (PSALM 127:2).

Peace and calmness in one's heart are never determined by outward circumstances. In his *Pax Vobiscum*, Henry Drummond said this: "Christ's life outwardly was one of the most troublous lives that was ever lived: tempest and tumult, tumult and tempest, the waves breaking over it all the time, until the warm body was laid in the grave. But the inner life was a sea of glass. The great calm was always there. At any time you might have gone to Him and found rest. Even when the bloodhounds were dogging Him in the streets of Jerusalem, He turned to His disciples and offered them as a last legacy, 'My peace.' Truly our Lord knew the God of the sparrows and of the lilies of the field."

Seek First the Kingdom

Then, as the climax of this word on how to overcome your anxiety, Jesus said, "But seek ye first the kingdom of God, and his righteousness; and all these things will be added unto you" (MATTHEW 6:33); that is, forget yourself. Lose your life in some great enterprise, and all of the things that you were so concerned about will be settled.

The other day, I was out playing golf with a man who is past sixty years old. We came to the end of eighteen holes, and he said, "I feel so good. Let's play nine holes more!" As we walked along, I said, "I am amazed by your physical strength. Have you always been as strong as you are?" He told me that when he started out in life, he was poor, and he was anxious to obtain financial security. He worked hard, and his business succeeded.

When he was fifty years old, he sold out everything he had and retired. He ended up with several millions of dollars, and all he had to do during the remainder of his life was collect the dividends from his investments. He did not have to worry about anything. After a short time, he found himself getting very nervous. He and his wife had made several trips to Europe and other places, but now he was fed up with traveling. He had reached the point where he had difficulty sleeping at night, and his appetite was not what it should have been. One day he had a heart attack. After that, his wife wanted him never to be alone, and wherever he went, somebody had to be with him. He was taking a handful of pills every day. He had become a sick and miserable man.

He decided, "I may die, but I'm not going to die like this!" He took all the money he had made, and borrowed that much more and invested it in the biggest venture he had ever undertaken. He stood a chance to lose everything, but he went back to work and threw himself wholeheartedly into it. This required getting up earlier, and staying up later, and giving all he had to his work. The new undertaking became a great success, and today that man is worth at least ten times as much as he was when he "retired." But that is not the important thing to him. Now he has his physical strength. He has peace in his mind. He can sleep and eat, and he gets fun out of living. Instead of taking a handful of pills every day, and having to have somebody watch him, now, at the end of eighteen holes of golf, he can say, "Let's play nine more!" What saved that man? Simply forgetting himself and throwing himself into a greater enterprise.

Jesus said, "Seek ye first the kingdom of God" (MAT-THEW 6:33). In another place He put it this way: "He that findeth his life shall lose it: and he that loseth his life for my sake shall find it" (MATTHEW 10:39). The principle is clear: Get yourself off your hands by giving yourself to something greater and bigger. The greatest enterprise in which we can engage ourselves is to know God, to love Him, to seek to make God's kingdom real in our own lives and in our world. Did not God create the universe, and does He not sustain it? Does not God cause the sun to rise in the morning, and the rain to fall upon the earth? Did not God establish the laws of nature and all of life? Has not God provided abundantly in every area in which man lives? THEREFORE, . . . *shall he not much more clothe you, O ye of little faith . . . ?*

Jesus is here laying down both a principle and a promise. The principle is: Fix your mind firmly on God; commit your life completely to His purposes. The promise is: All of the things that you need and really desire shall be provided for you. The Christian should reach the point St. Paul reached when he exclaimed, ". . . my God shall supply all your needs . . ." (PHILIPPIANS 4:19).

Judge Not

Judge not, that ye be not judged.

For with what judgment ye judge, ye shall be judged: and with what measure ye mete, it shall be measured to you again.

And why beholdest thou the mote that is in thy brother's eye, but considerest not the beam that is in thine own eye?

Or how wilt thou say to thy brother, Let me pull out the mote out of thine eye; and, behold, a beam is in thine own eye?

Thou hypocrite, first cast out the beam out of thine

148 ·

own eye; and then shalt thou see clearly to cast out the mote out of thy brother's eye (MATTHEW 7:1-5).

This is really one of the most frightening and disturbing passages in the Bible. It points its finger straight at each one of us and says, ". . . ye shall be judged." I do not know exactly what the judgment is like, but I do know that somehow, sometime, somewhere, it takes place. I cannot believe that Adolf Hitler and Albert Schweitzer are going to receive the same eternal treatment. If there is not a day of judgment, then the universe is not fair and God is not just.

Once a farmer wrote the editor of a newspaper: "Dear Mr. Editor: My neighbor goes to church and observes Sunday. I ploughed my fields on Sunday. I sowed my fields on Sunday. I harvested them on Sunday. Mr. Editor, at the end of the season and the end of the harvest, I did better than any of my neighbors who observed Sunday and went to church. How do you explain that?"

The editor's answer was brief. He wrote: "God doesn't make up His final account in October."

We may get along all right day by day. It may seem that evil triumphs. But then there comes the final judgment of God. ". . . ye shall be judged," said Jesus.

How shall we be judged? According to our sins? That is not what He said. He said, ". . . with what judgment ye judge . . . , with what measure ye mete. . . ." We will be judged according to our judgment of others. Knowing that Jesus spoke these words, why are we so quick to judge others? Let me note here five reasons why we pass judgment upon our fellow men:

(1) Being conscious of our own sins, we take comfort in someone else's fault. There are two ways to boost ourselves. One way is to live up to the highest and best of

which we are capable; the other way is to pull the other person down to our lower level. The latter way is much easier. Here is the reason why people like to repeat gossip: in comparison, it makes them feel better.

(2) We judge others because we are jealous. Often it is that secretly, in our hearts, we would like to be commiting the same sins we condemn. We suspect that the other person is having more fun than we are having. But we do not do as he does because we lack the nerve, or the opportunity, or our own conscience won't let us. Still, we resent the other person's doing these things. Often it is that the thing we most condemn is our own greatest desire or temptation.

(3) We judge others because we do not know all the facts and circumstances of their lives. On the cross, Jesus prayed, "Father, forgive them. . . ." Why did He pray that prayer? Because He knew the limitations of people's understanding. So He added, ". . . for they know not what they do" (LUKE 23:34). Surely it is that so many times we do not know what another person is doing. The ancient Rabbi Hillel said, "Do not judge a man until you yourself have come into his circumstances or situation." We cannot know the strength of another man's temptation.

(4) Judging others takes our minds off our own sins. It is a lot more comfortable to talk about the mistakes and wrongs of another's life than it is to face up to the wrongs of our own lives.

(5) We judge others quickly and harshly because we lack love in our hearts. When we love our fellow men, we will live the truth of this little verse:

Don't look for the faults as you go through life,
And even when you find them,

It's wise and kind to be somewhat blind,
And look for the virtues behind them.

There are two important reasons why we should be
very careful in our judgments. (1) We do not know all
of the facts, and therefore we cannot judge fairly and
impartially. According to the records, the Greeks held a
particularly important and difficult trial in the dark so
that the judge and jury could not see the man on trial;
they did not want them to be influenced by anything but
the facts in the case. The truth is that our judgments are
clouded and influenced by so many things, and it is almost impossible for us to look at another life and give an
unbiased verdict. Our judgments can be so wrong.

John Wesley tells of a man whom he had condemned
for many years. Wesley felt that the man was one of the
stingiest people he had ever known. He knew that the
man had a handsome income, yet he contributed very
little of it. On one occasion, when the man gave a very
small gift to one of Wesley's causes, Wesley criticized
the man very caustically. The man looked Wesley in the
eye and said, "I know a man who, at the week's beginning, goes to market and buys a few cents' worth of
parsnips, and takes them home to boil in water, and all
that week he has parsnips for his meat and the water for
his drink, and meat and drink alike cost him a few cents a
week."

"Who is the man?" asked Wesley.

"I am," was the reply.

Later, Wesley wrote in his journal these comments:
"This he constantly did, although he then had an adequate income, in order that he might pay the debt he had
contracted before he knew God. And this was the man
that I had thought to be covetous."

(2) The second reason we should not judge others is that we are not good enough. Very graphically our Lord pointed out this fact. He asked, "Why bother about the speck of dust in your brother's eye when there is a plank in your own eye?" To those who judge others, He says, "Thou hypocrites!" Before we start judging other people, we should be sure that our own lives are clean and pure and above reproach.

Before we express judgment against others, let's be sure that our judgment passes the three fold test: (1) Is it true? (2) Is it necessary? (3) Is it kind? And let us never forget a little poem that most of us have known since childhood:

> There is so much good in the worst of us,
> And so much bad in the best of us,
> That it hardly behooves any of us
> To talk about the rest of us.

George Waelis Koch

Frederick W. Faber wrote a wonderful hymn which begins:

> There's a wideness in God's mercy,
> Like the wideness of the sea;
> There's a kindness in His justice,
> Which is more than liberty.

In our hymnbooks, there is one verse of this hymn which is usually left out. It reads:

> There is no place where earth's sorrows
> Are more felt than up in heaven;

There is no place where earth's failings
Have such kindly judgment given.

Let us thank God for His mercy toward us, and let us extend that mercy to all those we meet.

Be Careful With the Holy

Give not that which is holy unto the dogs, neither cast ye your pearls before swine, lest they trample them under their feet, and turn again and rend you (MATTHEW 7:6).

In this verse the word "pearls" refers to the precious truths of the gospel. The word "cast" refers to the efforts of the disciples to present these precious truths to other people. The words "dogs" and "swine" refer to people who scoff at holy things. The meaning here is quite clear, and not as harsh as it first sounds. It simply means that there are some people who do not have the training, the background, the understanding to accept the truth of God. Before they can hear the gospel, something must happen to them within their hearts. There are some people so devoid of a sense of what is holy that they trample upon pearls. With these people it is useless to argue. Christians should learn that they can never win unsympathetic people by arguing about their faith.

Aristotle may have had the same thought in mind when he said, "Do not let your wisdom fall on the public highway." Many times I have sat with a small group of ministers as we discussed the faith. We have talked about things that puzzle and perplex us, and allowed our minds to speculate on the truths of God. Because of our training in the seminary and in our work, we could understand each other, whereas one who had not had the same training and experiences would not understand. A group of doctors can sit together and talk about things that one who is not a doctor would completely fail to comprehend. The same might be said of a group of lawyers, or people trained in any field. Also, this is true with Christians. Therefore, some truths which Christians share with each other are completely incomprehensible to one who has never experienced Christ. Thus, there are times when we make a mistake to offer to certain people certain truths concerning the Kingdom of God.

However, we do not give up on these people, and there is a better way. Dr. William Barclay records a discussion in a camp of young people where representatives of many nations were living together. They were discussing various ways of proclaiming the gospel. They turned to the girl from Africa. "Maria," they asked, "what do you do in your country?"

"Oh," said Maria, "we don't have preaching missions or pass out pamphlets. We just send one or two Christian families to live and work in a village, and when people see what Christians are like, then they want to be Christians, too."

There are times when we cannot win others through speaking the truth of God. Instead, we can impress them only as we live the truth of God. It may well be that the reason the Christian faith has not won the world up to now is not the lack of Christian argument, but, rather, the lack of Christian lives.

Persistence in Prayer

Ask, and it shall be given you; seek, and ye shall find;
knock, and it shall be opened unto you:
For every one that asketh receiveth; and he that seek-
eth findeth; and to him that knocketh it shall be opened.
Or what man is there of you, whom if his son ask
bread, will he give him a stone?
Or if he ask a fish, will he give him a serpent?
If ye then, being evil, know how to give good gifts
unto your children, how much more shall your Father
which is in heaven give good things to them that ask
him? (MATTHEW 7:7-11).

Many reasons are given as to why people do not pray,
such as: lack of faith, or not knowing how to pray, or
the knowledge that there are things in one's life that
make one ashamed to face God. None of these are the
real reasons for failure to pray. The real reason why
many people do not pray is simply that they have nothing to pray for. The supreme tragedy of many people's
lives is that they want so little and are satisfied with
almost nothing. They have no high dreams and lofty
hopes, no great ambitions and burning desires. Wanting
nothing, they pray for nothing. Too many people are
satisfied with life just as it is.

Someone asked Raphael, "Which is your greatest
painting?" He replied, "My next one." In contrast, consider the attitude of the president of the Pierce-Arrow
automobile company, who, in the year 1910, said, "We
have built the finest car it will ever be possible to build.
No improvements can ever be made." It has been a long

time now since the Pierce-Arrow car has been made.

Let some great need come into the life of any person, and he will naturally pray. To one who has need of prayer Jesus said, "Ask—seek—knock." In the original Greek, these three words are used in the present tense, and they call for continuing action. The better translation is: "Keep on asking—keep on seeking—keep on knocking."

The first step in prayer is *to ask*.

(1) To ask implies a sense of need and an admission of helplessness. The blind man on the corner asks for help. He is merely begging because he offers nothing in return, and before God there are times when we can only come asking. However, we are His children, and a child has the right to ask his father without shame.

(2) To ask means to apply to a person. A tree is beautiful, but one cannot ask a tree for anything because a tree cannot respond. To pray means that one must be conscious that there is a personal God who hears.

(3) To ask is to be definite. St. Paul said, ". . . let your requests be made known unto God" (PHILIPPIANS 4:6).

The second step in prayer is *to seek*. Seeking means asking plus effort. When Jesus told us to pray, *Give us this day our daily bread,* He did not mean that we are to expect God simply to rain down manna from heaven. Rather, this means *Give us the opportunity to earn our bread.* For the farmer, it means the opportunity to plow the field, and plant the seeds, and cultivate the crops. For others, it means the opportunity to use the money they have earned as a result of their labors to buy the bread. The prayer *Thy kingdom come* means that we commit ourselves to the task of building it. *To seek* means that to use what we have to answer our own prayers, expecting God to add to our resources.

The third step in prayer is to *knock*. Knocking is asking plus effort plus persistence. Jesus told the story of a man who continued to knock on his neighbor's door at midnight until the man inside got up and answered his request. Moffatt's translation has it: "I tell you, though he will not get up and give you anything because you are a friend of his, he will at least rise and give you whatever you want because you persist" (LUKE 11:5-8).

In another place Jesus said, ". . . men ought always to pray, and not to faint" (LUKE 18:1). To faint means to quit. One may allow bitterness or disappointment or lack of understanding or hopelessness to turn him away from God. How long must one keep on praying? Until the answer comes. Earlier in the Sermon on the Mount, Jesus said, . . . *your Father knoweth what things ye have need of, before ye ask him* (MATTHEW 6:8). But it is often true that we ourselves do not know what we need, and God mercifully withholds His answer until we come with the right request. God may say "No" to our request, but that is no reason for us to stop praying. We must continue to pray until we get God's "Yes." A dear mother told me how she prayed for the safety of her son, who was on the battlefield. Her request was definite and persistent, yet the boy was killed. But she did not stop praying. She kept on until the bitterness was taken out of her heart, and until she found a strengthening and comforting fellowship with God. So, Jesus points out, just as a father would not give his son a stone when he asked for bread, the heavenly Father will give his children "good things to them that ask him."

We remember that when Augustine was a youth, he wanted to go to Rome. Rome was a wild and wicked city, and his mother, Monica, prayed persistently that her son would be prevented from going to that place.

However, one day she stood on the shore and saw a ship sailing away, bearing her son to Rome. She might have felt that God had refused to hear and answer her prayer. However, she did not stop praying for her boy. In Rome, Augustine heard a great sermon and was converted and became one of the saints of the church. Suppose Monica had stopped praying when she received the answer "No"? Her real prayer was not that her son might be prevented from going to Rome. Rather was it that her son might become the Christian that he did become. Her real prayer was answered with a "Yes," but along the pathway of her prayer she received some answers which were "No." We are never to stop praying until we get the "Yes" answer.

The Nine Prayer Steps

To make the most of prayer, let me suggest nine prayer steps.

There are three steps to take *before* prayer:

(1) Decide what you really want. Get clearly in mind exactly what you plan to ask in prayer.

(2) Seek to determine whether or not what you want is right. Ask yourself such questions as: Is it fair to everyone else concerned? Is it best for me? Is it in harmony with the Spirit of God?

(3) Write it down. Reducing our requests to writing helps to clarify our thinking and deepen the impressions upon our mind and heart.

Then, there are three steps to take *during* prayer:

(1) Keep the mind still. Just as the moon cannot be perfectly reflected on a restless sea, so God cannot be experienced by an unquiet mind. "Be still, and know that

I am God" (PSALM 46:10). At this point we must concentrate to keep the mind from wandering. There are some books I cannot read while in a comfortable chair, and there are some prayers I cannot pray without being completely at attention. This is what Jesus meant when He said, ". . . when thou hast shut thy door . . ." (MATTHEW 6:6); that is, shut out distracting thoughts.

(2) Talk *with* God, and not *to* God. Instead of saying, with Samuel, "Speak; for thy servant heareth" (I SAMUEL 3:10), we are prone to say, "Listen, Lord, for Thy servant speaketh." Prayer is both speaking and listening.

(3) Promise God what you yourself will do to answer your own prayer. God answers prayer, not for you, but with you. Jesus performed many of His miracles by giving the person to be helped something to do. As you pray, search for the things that you yourself can do.

Then, there are three steps to take *after* prayer:

(1) Always remember to thank God for answering your prayer. You would not pray in the first place if you did not believe God would answer. Now, confirm that belief by thanking Him for the answer, even though it has not yet come.

(2) Be willing to accept whatever God's answer may be, remembering the words of our Lord, ". . . nevertheless not my will, but thine, be done" (LUKE 22:42).

(3) Do everything loving that comes to your mind. One of the objects of prayer is to bring the love of God into our hearts; and as we express that love, we make it possible for God to answer our prayers better.

The Golden Rule

Therefore all things whatsoever ye would that men should do to you, do ye even so to them: for this is the law and the prophets (MATTHEW 7:12).

A man was telling me about some people who had cheated him, talked about him, and wronged him in many ways. As a result, he felt deep resentment. He had collected grudges in the way that some people collect old coins or stamps. Finally, he said, "I am going to make people treat me right."

I pointed out to him that since he had not succeeded in making people treat him right, probably he was employing the wrong techniques. I suggested to him that there was one sure way of making people treat him right. When Tsze-Kung, a disciple of Confucius, asked his master, "Is there one word which may serve as a rule for all of one's life?" Confucius answered, "Is not 'reciprocity' such a word? What you do not want done to yourself, do not do to others."

Jesus stated the rule of reciprocity in positive terms which we have recorded in the Sermon on the Mount. We have shortened it to read simply: "Do unto others as you would have them do unto you." We call this the Golden Rule.

What would we like other people to do to us? Jesus' answer is simply: "Do not wait for them to do it to you. Do it to them first."

Here we find expressed one of the basic laws of the universe. Stand at the seashore, and watch the tide go out and the tide come in. There is no power on earth great enough to stop the tide, and that principle operates all through life: what goes out, comes in. Send out love, and love comes back. Send out hate—hate comes back. Send out mercy—mercy comes back. What we give, we get.

A man and his wife, both blind, were being interviewed on a radio program. They told of their baby, and of the joy they received from their baby's smile. The interviewer asked, "How do you know the baby smiles at you?"

The mother replied, "We never see the baby smile, that is true. And yet, when we send out our love to our baby, we can feel it coming back. We are as certain of her smile as though we could see it with our eyes."

One of the basic laws of physics is that, for every action, there is a corresponding reaction. That is also a law of life.

Let us consider three things which we want from others:

(1) We want people to like us, and, in liking us, to take a real interest in our lives. Nobody wants to be ignored. One of the saddest lines in the Bible is: ". . . no man cared for my soul" (PSALM 142:4). But in order for people to like us, they must distinguish between our real selves and some of our actions.

A friend of mine and I went out to lunch together and we both ordered hamburgers. I ordered onions on mine. As I ate it, he said, "I do not like onions on a hamburger." I would not want that man to dislike me simply because I was eating something he did not like. Sometimes I do things that people do not like; but I do not want them to dislike me for that reason. Some of the things I have done, I do not like myself, and I am ashamed of them.

When Will Rogers said, "I never met a man I did not

like," he did not mean that he liked everything about every person he met; but he looked beyond to the real person and, in liking the real person, he himself became one of the best-liked men in the history of our country. The Golden Rule works. If you want to be liked, begin by liking others.

(2) Another thing we want is for people to overlook our faults and forgive our failures. One thinks of Abraham Lincoln. Many wonderful things have been said about him, but the appraisal of Lincoln selected to be carved on his tomb in Springfield is this: "Now he belongs to the ages." Do you know who said that about Lincoln? It was Edwin M. Stanton—the same Stanton who once referred to Lincoln as "this great ignoramus from Illinois, a baboon who doesn't have brains enough to be the President." But Lincoln kept Stanton in office because, as he himself said, "He is the greatest Secretary of War we ever had." Lincoln looked beyond Stanton's faults and saw his real abilities. Eventually, Stanton did the same for Lincoln.

I know a man who keeps an ordinary rock on his desk. He is very careful to keep it in plain view and within easy reach. He does not keep it there for the purpose of hitting someone. On the contrary, it is there to stop him when he is tempted to hit someone with a criticism, to judge too quickly, or to return evil for evil. That man was deeply moved by the story of one who had done wrong and the crowd who would have stoned her to death. He keeps the stone on his desk so that, when he is tempted to stone one, it is a reminder of Jesus' words: "He that is without sin among you, let him first cast a stone at her" (JOHN 8:7). If you want to be forgiven, first you must forgive.

(3) Another thing we want from people is apprecia-

tion. There is nothing vain or childish about that; it is a longing of every human heart. We remember how ten lepers once came to Jesus, begging for healing. He quickly and freely used His power in their behalf. Only one of the ten took time to come back and say, "Thank You." Surely there was disappointment and grief in the Master's voice as He said, "Were there not ten cleansed? but where are the nine?" (LUKE 17:17). The Golden Rule works here, too. To get appreciation, begin by giving it.

Some have even said, "The Golden Rule is my religion." Those who say that make a serious mistake, because the Golden Rule is not a religion; it is merely an expression of religion. Without the religious experience, the expression is meaningless. Notice carefully that Jesus said, "Therefore, all things. . . ." The foundation of the Golden Rule is that "therefore."

Let us remember that these words come immediately after the section of the Sermon on the Mount in which Jesus had been talking about prayer. Prayer, literally, is the experiencing of the presence of God. Before man can be right with his fellow men, he must first be right with God. No one can live the Golden Rule without God in his heart and his life.

So, the conclusion of the matter is this: first, get right with God; second, treat your fellow men right; third, your fellow men will then treat you right.

The Narrow Way

Enter ye in at the strait gate: for wide is the gate, and broad is the way, that leadeth to destruction, and many there be which go in thereat:

· 163

Because strait is the gate, and narrow is the way, which leadeth unto life, and few there be that find it (MATTHEW 7:13-14).

The description of the Christian life as the "strait-and-narrow-way" is offensive to a lot of people. We pride ourselves on being "broadminded," and we resent being called "narrowminded." The narrow way is so unattractive that Jesus said, ". . . few there be that find it." Let us begin with the question: Why do many people refuse the narrow way?

(1) Some refuse the narrow way because of the people who profess to walk it. There are some who are negatively good. Their emphasis is merely on the sins they do not commit, and they have kept the lid clamped so tightly on their badness that they have become dried up and sour. Then there are those who are critically good. Their religion is strictly for export: to be applied to somebody else. They are always meddling with other people's lives. Then there are the narrowly good. They make a great to-do about insignificant matters of behavior, and miss all the great issues of life. Believing such people as these to be Christians, it is no wonder many people are not attracted to their ways. Such "good" people become an embarrassment to God's larger purpose.

(2) Some refuse the narrow way because they believe Christ was wrong. Many believe that life can best be found in certain forbidden pleasures, and in escaping certain hard duties. Evil often promises more pleasure than good. St. Paul tells us that "Satan himself is transformed into an angel of light" (II CORINTHIANS 11:14).

There are three main reasons why certain things are forbidden to those who follow Christ. First, our doing it may do harm to some other person. In the words of St. Paul, ". . . if meat make my brother to offend, I will eat no flesh . . ." (I CORINTHIANS 8:13). We are our brother's keeper, and that responsibility somewhat restricts our lives. Second, some things are forbidden because they degrade our souls. Third, most things which are forbidden are forbidden because they knock us out of something better. Often the Christian denies himself simply because he has more important things to do. The Christian is so concerned about the right, and so completely gives himself to the right, that he has no time or desire for the wrong.

It has been well said that God never threatens, the devil never warns. In this fashion Jesus is emphatically stating that the broad way leads to destruction and the narrow way leads to life. Here He is giving us both a warning and a promise.

First, consider the warning. The other day, I flew over a swamp. The plane was low enough so that one could see clearly the water below; it was covered with an ugly green film. That swamp is a breeding place for mosquitoes and vermin of many kinds. There was nothing attractive about it, and it certainly was not an area where one would want to spend much time. That swamp is fed by a creek that runs up into the mountains. I am quite familiar with that creek because a number of times I have been up it fishing for rainbow trout. It is a beautiful creek, clear and sparkling and pure. Up in the mountains it runs in a rather narrow bed, and many times it is compelled to flow over rocks and rough places. As it flows on down out of hills into the lowlands, the creek says to itself, "I am tired to this restricted narrow life I have been forced to live. I want to spread out and take in more territory." But, in spreading out, it ceases to be the clear, pure creek and becomes a contaminated swamp.

There are those who have said, "I resent restraint and repression. I want to do as I please. I want to let myself go." But usually it is the wrong self that they want to let go. Life would be much simpler if man were just a single self. The truth is, we are many selves. There is our passionate self, and our greedy self, and our careless self, and our best self. The prodigal son "let himself go," and ended up in a hog pen. Then we read, "And when he came to himself . . ." (LUKE 15:17)—just which of his selves are we to suppose that he came to? Afterward he went back to his father to say, ". . . make me as one of thy hired servants" (v. 19). That certainly does not indicate freedom or broadening out. He became willing to come back to the narrow way.

Second, let us put the emphasis upon our Lord's promise that the narrow way "leadeth unto life." That is why we choose that way—because it leads somewhere. Recently, I was in another city for some speaking engagements. When my work there was finished, I went to the airport to buy a ticket. I did not say to the people, "I am broadminded; I will go anywhere." I wanted a ticket only to Houston, Texas, because that is where I live. It was after midnight when I arrived in Houston. Often I enjoy driving through the city, but that night I told the taxi-driver that I wanted to go to River Oaks. When we got to that residential area, I did not say to the man, "There are many lovely houses here; just drop me at any one of them." I told him I wanted to go to a specific street and a specific house on that street. By being narrow, I arrived in my own home.

Certainly "narrow is the way" for the mathematician. There is nothing liberal about the multiplication table: two times two is four, never five or three. This law also

166 ·

applies to the musician: harmony is produced by obedience to strict laws; when the musician breaks one of those laws, he ends up with discord. Certainly the principle of the narrow way was true for our Lord. His path was so narrow that when He came to a cross, there was no room to go around it. Yet, who will deny the fact that He really found life; and the principle of the narrow way is true for every person who would find life.

We have two kinds of freedom, the freedom to do what we want to do, and the freedom to do what we ought to do. It is in exercising our freedom to do what we ought to do that we really find life. We sing, in the hymn "America the Beautiful," these words:

> Confirm thy soul in self-control
> Thy liberty in law.

George Washington was free to be at ease in Virginia. He was also free to go to Valley Forge. Lincoln was free to live in a small town in Illinois. He was also free to suffer the heartbreak of a nation. Albert Schweitzer was free to live in Europe. He was also free to give his life in healing the wounds in the Congo.

There is a Scottish proverb: "A stoot hairt to tae a stae brae"; it means: "A strong heart to a difficult hill." Let us always keep in mind that the Christian life is a holy life, and we make a mistake when we substitute the word "happy" for "holy." The Christian happiness comes only as a consequence of holiness. The strait-and-narrow way means pure and holy living. Happiness is not what the Christian seeks, but rather the result that follows the holy life.

Mark Twain wrote brilliantly, and achieved wonderful success. Then he lost his fortune and tumbled into deep debt. Some of his friends urged him to take the easy way out and escape his responsibilities by going into bankruptcy. He refused, and instead, although he was now an old man, he threw himself into tirelessly speaking and writing until the last penny was paid. He summed up the reasons for his actions in one graphic sentence: "Honor is a harder master than the law." In the end, who would not say that Mark Twain on the hard way found a greater happiness and a greater life.

But the one who walks the narrow way is not narrow altogether. He is broad both in his love and in his hope. It is the Christian who can truly sing the popular song, "Don't Fence Me In." It is prejudice which builds social and racial and national fences. It is love that reaches out in compassionate understanding to all men everywhere. It is sympathy that bridges all the chasms that separate humanity. The Christian is so broad that he can carry upon his heart the weight of the world's hurt. The Christian is broad in that he gives himself to the building of the Kingdom of God throughout the whole world, and there is nothing broader and more encompassing than that.

Broad in his hopes, too, is the one who walks the narrow way. Life on this earth is so limited and small, the one who is living merely for this life can hope for perhaps only seventy or eighty years. The Christian hopes for life where a thousand years are but a day. On the narrow way one finds life that makes him glad even in death. And so let us sing the great hymn of George Matheson:

> Make me a captive, Lord,
> And then I shall be free;
> Force me to render up my sword,

And I shall conqueror be.
I sink in life's alarms
When by myself I stand;
Imprison me within Thine arms,
And strong shall be my hand.

False Prophets

Beware of false prophets, which come to you in sheep's clothing, but inwardly they are ravening wolves.

Ye shall know them by their fruits. Do men gather grapes of thorns, or figs of thistles?

Even so every good tree bringeth forth good fruit; but a corrupt tree bringeth forth evil fruit.

A good tree cannot bring forth evil fruit, neither can a corrupt tree bring forth good fruit.

Every tree that bringeth not forth good fruit is hewn down, and cast into the fire.

Wherefore by their fruits ye shall know them (MATTHEW 7:15-20).

Here is a passage to test the life of the preacher, the Christian, and the church. "Wolves in sheep's clothing" is a very descriptive sentence. In Jesus' day, the shepherd wore garments made of sheepskin. The sheep very quickly learned to recognize the shepherd by his appearance. Knowing the shepherd to be one who always wanted to help the sheep and never hurt them, the sheep were never afraid when the shepherd approached. In that day, there were many wild animals lurking about, looking for a chance to devour the sheep. The most feared of those animals were the wolves. If a sheep saw a wolf, it would run, and bleat, and take every possible measure to protect itself. Suppose a wolf could be dressed in the clothing of the shepherd? It is possible that the sheep might be so fooled by the appearance that it would fail to be on guard, and would be destroyed.

Here our Lord uses a very extreme analogy to point out a very common fault. The fault is simply appearing to be something that we are not. The matter He is dealing with is insincerity.

The word "sincerity" comes from a combination of two Latin words: *sine*, which means "without," and *cera*, which means "wax." In the days of the Roman Empire, marble was one of the finest materials with which to build. Even today, Italian marble is noted for its fineness and beauty. In those early days, when a piece of marble had a defective seam in it, there were certain unscrupulous people who would carefully cover that defect with wax, and sell the marble as a perfect stone. Honest dealers would label their marble *sine-cera*—that is, "without wax." They were saying that the piece of marble was exactly as it appeared to be.

We do no violence to the words of our Lord in Matthew 7:15 when we translate them to read: "Beware of insincere people." Truly this must be one of the first qualities of the Christian. Suppose some angel were to come to one of us and offer any treasure our heart may desire—wealth, position, popularity, influence, prestige— but, in return for any one of these gifts, or even all of them, we would have to give up our sincerity; that is, we would have to appear to be something that we are not. We would be compelled to dress our lives with sham. We just could not afford to trade. I know of nothing that destroys the influence of one's life more quickly and completely than insincerity.

Insincerity is the one thing the world will not forgive

the Christian. Through the years, I have learned in my own experience that people will forgive me for not being perfect. I know that in the Sermon on the Mount Jesus tells us to *"Be ye therefore perfect . . ."* (MATTHEW 5:48). This should be the goal toward which every one of us is striving; but the fact remains, none of us has yet reached that stage in our lives. With shame, I say that I have done some things and said some things that were wrong. At times, I have made obvious errors in grammar in my sermons. In some of my decisions on behalf of the church, I have used bad judgment. Across the years, I can name undertakings into which I have entered in the church, and which ended in failure. My life and my ministry have certainly seen many failures. I am sure that I have preached some dull sermons, but thank God for the mercy and charitable love of people! One reason that I have such confidence in the forgiving mercy of God is that I have received that same forgiving mercy from so many people across the years. This is true of all of us. We have all been forgiven by our fellow men time and time again. But one thing which people will not forgive is insincerity. The world demands of the preacher and of every Christian that we be what we appear to be.

And how does the world judge the sincerity of the Christian? By what we say we are? No. By the results of our lives—*"by their fruits ye shall know them."*

The Fruits of the
Christian Life

St. Paul tells us that "the fruit of the Spirit is love, joy, peace, longsuffering, gentleness, goodness, faith, Meekness, temperance . . ." (GALATIANS 5:22-23). If a person really has Christ in his heart, then this wonderful list of virtues will appear in his life. One could comment at length upon the fruits which Paul named, but just the reading of that list is enough to indict most of us, and send us to our knees in repentance.

Once, when David Hume was asked why he went to hear a certain man preach, he replied, "I do not go to hear him because I believe what he says. I hear him because he believes what he says." Sincerity is the one virtue that wins the respect of our fellow men.

(1) If one who seeks to represent Christ is truly sincere, he will throw himself completely and unreservedly into his task. The expression "half-hearted Christians" is really a contradiction in terms. The Christian may fail again and again, but one cannot imagine a Christian not wholeheartedly trying.

Once an atheist said to a Christian, "If I believed what you say you believe, I would crawl on my hands and knees to tell other people about it."

Charles Wesley expressed the spirit of the Christian in a verse of one of his hymns:

> Happy if with my latest breath
> I may but gasp His name;
> Preach Him to all, and cry in death,
> Behold, behold the Lamb!

One of the severest temptations of the minister is idleness. One of the things he must learn is the value of time. Benjamin Franklin's words should never be forgotten: "Value time, for time is the stuff of which life is made." On the tombstone of many people could be written the reason for their failure in just these words: "He

172 ·

dawdled." And we need to remember that one can be very busy, and yet fail to be busy with the right things. One of our constant temptations is to give our time and energy to smaller things.

(2) Another proof of the Christian life is patience. Now, there are some things about which a Christian is very impatient. He is impatient about the wrongs in the community. But the Christian learns to be patient about results. Too often we get discouraged when we have done our best and fail to see the results that we want and expect. Let us remember the words of St. Paul: ". . . let us not be weary in well doing: for in due season we shall reap, if we faint not" (GALATIANS 6:9); and also these words of the Apostle: "Therefore, my beloved brethren, be ye stedfast, unmoveable, always abounding in the word of the Lord, forasmuch as ye know that your labour is not in vain in the Lord" (I CORINTHIANS 15:58). This is one of the things that I myself have had to fight the hardest. When I work at something with all I have, and do not get results, I have a tendency to become discouraged. In recent years, we have seen a number of articles on the subject "Why I Quit the Ministry." The gist of what most of these men say is simply that they did not get the results they expected. But the Christian learns to leave the results to God, knowing that what he does in His name is "not in vain."

(3) Another fruit of Christian life is witnessing at every opportunity. One of our temptations is to say that we would be happy to stand in a great pulpit somewhere and speak to multitudes, to have the opportunities of radio and television, to write our witness for some great metropolitan newspaper, to write books which would be read by thousands of people. But such opportunities are given to relatively few people. In the meantime, let us

remember that Jesus spoke His message on the new birth to just one man, Nicodemus. Let us remember that He spoke some of the greatest truths ever spoken in reference to eternity to just one woman, Martha. A long time ago, someone said, "Winning people one at a time is the best way of winning the world in time." Daily we come in contact with persons to whom we can give our witness if there really is the desire in our hearts.

(4) There are many other fruits of the Christian life, but here let me mention one more. The Christian always sounds the positive and hopeful note. One trouble with the Pharisees was that they gave the impression of merely being against something. I have never understood why it is that we are much more zealous in reference to the things we are against than the things we are for. It is much easier to organize crusades against evil than in behalf of righteousness, but the Christian has a positive Christ to present to the world. Someone has said that a pessimist is one who sees difficulty in every opportunity, and an optimist is one who sees opportunity in every difficulty. We never change the world by weeping and wailing about all that is wrong. Instead, the Christian seeks the answer, and proclaims it with joy and optimistic faith. The real test of any preaching is: Does it strengthen the person and help him to bear the burdens of life?

V

V

The Test of the Christian Life

Hearing and Doing

*Not every one that saith unto me, Lord, Lord, shall
enter into the kingdom of heaven; but he that doeth the
will of my Father which is in heaven.*

*Many will say to me in that day, Lord, Lord, have we
not prophesied in thy name? and in thy name have cast
out devils? and in thy name done many wonderful
works?*

*And then will I profess unto them, I never knew you:
depart from me, ye that work inequity.*

*Therefore whosoever heareth these sayings of mine,
and doeth them. . . .* (MATTHEW 7:21-24).

IN A THEOLOGICAL seminary the students will
often preach in the chapel services. Later, they will go to
some of the professors for constructive criticism. Once,
after a sermon, a certain student went to a professor to
hear his comments. The professor sat silently for a time,
and finally the student anxiously asked, "My sermon will
do, won't it?" The professor replied, "It will do what?"

Sermons must say something, but also they must do something. In the Sermon on the Mount, Jesus set down the important principles of the Christian faith, truths that the disciples should hear and learn well. It is important to learn, to gain knowledge, but that is never the end of the matter. Somewhere I read the story of a man nearly seventy years old who is a student in Columbia University. The fact is that he has spent upwards of fifty years as a student in this university. His father had stipulated in his will that his son was to receive $300 a month as long as he was a student in college. So the man just stayed in school, taking every course that was offered. He has learned a lot about many things and gained a number of degrees; he is probably one of the most knowledgeable men of his day; but, who can say that such a life is a success? The purpose in going to school is to be able to go out in life and live the things that one has learned.

It is important to hear the truth in a sermon, but any sermon is a failure if all it does is inform. Beyond teaching the truth, the sermon should do three things: (1) It should stir our feelings. I know there are some people who feel we should leave emotion out of religion, but they are mistaken. When one hears the truth of God it should stir his heart. (2) A sermon should stimulate one's mind. We read in the Bible: "Come now, and let us reason together . . ." (ISAIAH 1:18). Without reins on the horse, he would run wild; and without reason and intelligent thinking, our emotions would get out of hand. But a sermon should do more than cause us to feel and to think. (3) The sermon must inspire some action. Every sermon should begin with truth and end in life.

Once a boy was carrying eggs to market in a basket. He stumbled and fell, and all the eggs were broken. People gathered around and expressed sympathy for him.

One said, "You poor little boy. I'm sorry for you. What a pity you broke your eggs." Then another man stepped up and said, "I'm sorry the little boy broke his eggs, and I'm sorry fifty-cents worth." Another man was sorry "a quarter's worth," and another expressed his sorrow, and still another, until finally the boy had enough money in hand to pay for the eggs.

It's good to have an emotion, but an emotion is not worth much if it does not result in action. We come away from church saying, "That was a fine service." Well, how good a service was it? Good enough to make you pay some old debt? Control a temper? Put a bridle on your tongue? Be pleasant at home? Be honest in business? Stop using profane language? Do your part in the Lord's work? It is one thing to desire the salvation of the world; it is another thing to dedicate a rightful share of your time, talent, and money to help do it.

I sometimes think that if Jesus were present in the flesh today, He might wonder why we have built such magnificent church buildings, and He might become confused in some of our intricate worship services. In a church where I was once pastor, there were two candles immediately in front of the pulpit. I did not care much for them, so one week I just took them out. The following Sunday a number of people expressed deep indignation because the candles had been removed. It appeared that, for some of them, the burning of the candles in the church was the most important activity. I think Jesus would not really care whether or not we had any candles burning in our churches. He probably would be bored listening to some of the theological debates in which Christians engage.

If Christ were here today, we may be sure that He would re-emphasize His words: "He that doeth the will of My Father." This is not to say that He would preach salvation by works—far from it. Let us emphasize the fact that we are saved through faith. Let us remember also that faith without works is dead. In the second chapter of his Epistle, James felt that this was so important that he stated it three times. Certainly this is in harmony with the Spirit of Christ. Study His teachings and you will see how often He stresses the fact that those who are saved do something about it. In the story of the ten virgins, the wise virgins were admitted because they did something about the matter of oil for their lamps. In the parable of the talents, the ones who were commended were the ones who used their talents. The man who buried his talent in the ground was severely condemned. In the parable of the Good Samaritan, the priest and Levite were condemned because they simply passed by on the other side and did nothing for the wounded man. Jesus did not say, "Well *thought*, thou good and faithful servant. Thou hast heard well and thy emotions have been stirred. Enter thou into the joy of thy Lord." He said, "Well *done*, thou good and faithful servant . . ." (MATTHEW 25:21).

It is one thing to read the words of the Scripture, select sentences here and there, and set them up as little slogans for our lives. But it is quite a different thing to take the truths of God and spend the rest of your days trying to match those truths in your life. The Christian knows that it is not what he says, but what he does, that counts.

During a bitter debate in his cabinet, Abraham Lincoln once stopped to ask what seemed to be an almost foolish question. He asked, "How many legs would a sheep have if you say that the tail is a leg?" One of the cabinet members spoke up and said, "if you say the tail is a leg, then the sheep would have five legs." Then Lincoln replied, "No. Just to say the tail is a leg does not make it so."

A lot of people think that just to speak the truths of God is enough. The truths of God never become real for us until they become part of our actions and our lives. And while I have pointed out that we do not believe in salvation by works, I think our works have more to do with our salvation than we know. Someone has said that if a man were to do before he got religion what he would do if he had religion, then he would get religion.

Two generations ago, Dr. Hugh Price Hughes was one of the great preachers of London. In that day, Charles Bradlaugh, a famous atheist, challenged the great preacher to a public debate. Hughes agreed to debate, with the following provisions: he would bring a hundred people who had been redeemed by the Spirit of Christ as witnesses to the Christian faith, and Bradlaugh was to bring a hundred pagans who had found satisfaction in their godless way of life. The hall was filled to capacity on the night of the debate. Dr. Hughes was there with his hundred people, but Bradlaugh never did show up. He could debate the preacher as long as they used arguments; but when they began using lives, he was defeated. As long as we simply talk to the world, we will never win, but when we begin showing the world our lives which have been redeemed by the Christ, then the world cannot argue back.

One of Edgar A. Guest's poems should be repeated here:

I'd rather see a sermon than hear one any day!
I'd rather one should walk with me than merely tell
    the way.

The eye's a better pupil and more willing than the ear,
Fine counsel is confusing but example's always clear.
I soon can learn to do it, if you'll let me see it
    done;
I can watch your hands in action, but your tongue
    too fast may run,
And the lecture you deliver may be very wise and true,
But I'd rather get my lesson by observing what you do;
For I might misunderstand you and the high advice you
    give,
But there's no misunderstanding how you act and how
    you live.

For many years, I have felt that the most important moment in a church service was not during the anthem, or the pastoral prayer, or the offering, or even the sermon. I think the height of any church service is the final hymn. I always select that last hymn with great care. The worshiper has been inspired by the service and has heard the Word of God in the sermon. Now, during the last hymn, is the time for him to make a response, a decision, to determine a course of action, and without this commitment on the part of the worshiper, then the service is in vain.

Jesus is described as One "who went about doing good . . ." (ACTS 10:38). And, if we would be His followers, we, too, must go about doing good.

Houses on Rock and Sand

Therefore whosoever heareth these sayings of mine, and doeth them, I will liken him unto a wise man, which built his house upon a rock:

*And the rain descended, and the floods came, and the
winds blew, and beat upon that house; and it fell not: for
it was founded upon a rock.*

*And every one that heareth these sayings of mine, and
doeth them not, shall be likened unto a foolish man,
which built his house upon the sand:*

*And the rain descended, and the floods came, and the
winds blew, and beat upon that house; and it fell: and
great was the fall of it* (MATTHEW 7:24-27).

Jesus begins the conclusion of the Sermon with the
word "therefore." A dozen times He uses that word
throughout the Sermon to drive home particular points.
He uses it to magnify the importance of the Law, to
emphasize the spirit of giving, twice to condemn show or
display in religious practices, twice to stress the value of
following the light, three times to warn against undue
anxiety, and once to sum up the arguments for the
Golden Rule. One could preach a sermon on the "there-
fores" in the Sermon on the Mount. The last "therefore"
does not refer to any specific point of the Sermon, but is
used to gather it all up and lead into the conclusion of the
whole truth.

(1) He likens the building of one's life to the building
of houses. One can build either on the rocks or on the
sand. The sand to which he was referring was in the wide
river beds in Palestine. These beds were made by melting
snows coming down from the mountains. Maybe only
once in a generation would the snows be so heavy as to
cause floods as they melted; most of the time there were
nice little streams trickling down through the bottom of
the wide bed. The sand was an easy and delightful place
on which to build. The water was nearby, and the house
was sheltered from the cold winds of winter.

To build on the rocks was difficult. It meant grading the side of the hill and carrying up the materials. Also, living on the rocks was harder. The water had to be "toted," and the cold winter winds were more than a match for the poor fuel used in that day to warm the houses.

So it is with the building of a life. To build on the principles which Jesus taught in the Sermon on the Mount is not easy. It is never easy to keep your heart pure, to pray for those who have done you wrong, to return good for evil. When Jesus prayed, "Thy will be done," drops of blood popped out on His forehead; and it is also a deep struggle for us to pray those same words as He taught us to do. Self-denial is never easy. And the narrow way is not the most inviting. One feels deeply the temptation to lay up treasures upon earth and forget the treasures in heaven. We shrink from the command, "Be ye therefore perfect." To trust in God and not worry about what we shall eat and drink and wear, and the other physical needs of life, is easier said than done. The voice of inclination is always more alluring than the command of duty.

Never did Jesus say, "Come ye after Me, and I will make your life easy." He never put a carpet on the race-track, or a bed of roses on the battlefield. He talked about how one is persecuted for living the Christian Way. So we are not surprised when men turn from His Way to the easy, drifting life.

The first point Jesus would have us consider is the fact that we all are builders.

(2) The second point is that one of these days we are to be tested. It may be that the man who built his house down on the sand will get by for many years, but one year there will come an unusually heavy snow and a

quick thaw in the spring. At the same time there will be heavy spring rainstorms, and the water will come rushing down across the sand, destroying the houses built there. But the houses built higher up on the rocks will stand firm through the rains and the floods.

Tests come to our lives in many ways. There is discouragement, for example. We plan carefully; we work hard; and the success which we so highly prize eludes our grasp. We see others succeeding while we are failing.

There is the test of perplexity. "Why do the good suffer?" This is a question that is constantly upon the lips of men. One whom we love dearly is suddenly stricken with cancer or some other dread disease. Parents give their very best in the rearing and training of a son, only to have him break their hearts; the dreams they dreamed for their son are dashed to pieces. There are so many heartbreaking situations that arise in life, and which we cannot explain.

Added to the test of discouragement and perplexity is the test of bewilderment. We do not know which way to turn. There are so many problems for which we do not have the answer, decisions that we have difficulty in making.

Christians are never exempt from the test of temptation, and, in spite of our faith, at times the flood of anxiety comes sweeping over our lives. For many righteous and devout people, life becomes a hard struggle. There are financial setbacks; there is deep loneliness; there are physical pains; there are broken hearts.

Also, there is the test of the final judgment of God. One of the parables of Jesus describes a wheatfield with tares growing in it. The owner of the field did not go and root up the tares because to do so would also have rooted up the wheat. Instead, he said, "Let both grow together until the harvest: and in the time of harvest I will say to the reapers, Gather ye together first the tares, and bind them in bundles to burn them: but gather the wheat into my barn" (MATTHEW 13:30). Sometimes we wonder why God allows certain people and certain wrongs to live in His world. At times, it seems the causes of evil prosper the most, and wrong does appear to be on the throne: but we know that God has the final word.

St. Paul summed it all up in these words: "For other foundation can no man lay than that is laid, which is Jesus Christ" (I CORINTHIANS 3:11). In the words of the gospel song:

> On Christ, the solid Rock, I stand;
> All other ground is sinking sand.

One Having Authority

And it came to pass, when Jesus had ended these sayings, the people were astonished at his doctrine:

For he taught them as one having authority, and not as the scribes (MATTHEW 7:28-29).

After the Sermon on the Mount was concluded, Matthew added the above words. At the beginning, we pointed out that Jesus spoke these words to the disciples. It may be that some of the people followed them up on the mount and overheard the Master speaking. Or, it may be that Matthew was thinking of the response of the people on many occasions when Jesus spoke directly to them. Either way, he felt it worthy of record to point out the response of the people. They were accustomed to hearing their own scribes, whose words consisted primarily of what their scholars had said, and there was very little force or power in those words. But, as Jesus spoke, they heard a new voice that amazed them, both by what He said, and the Spirit and power in which He said it. He did not speak citing the words and authority of others, but spoke as one having authority within Himself. It was an astonishing thing to hear Someone talk who knew what He was talking about, and those who heard Him were deeply impressed.

Though we cannot see His facial expressions and hear the tone of His voice today, still, even from the cold type of the printed page as we read His words, we, too, recognize Him "as one having authority." Blessed be those who give to Him authority over their lives.